The Complete Riding and Driving System
BOOK 1

The Principles of Riding

The Official Handbook of The
German National Equestrian Federation

The Kenilworth Press Limited
Threshold Books

© FN-Verlag der Deutschen Reiterlichen Vereinigung
GmbH approves this edition of 'Richtlinien für Reiten
und Fahren, Band 1'

English language edition © 1985 and 1990 The Kenilworth Press Limited

Threshold Books
The Kenilworth Press Limited
Addington
Buckingham MK18 2JR

Reprinted 1987, 1991

Translation and additional illustrations by **Gisela Holstein**
Consultant **Jane Kidd**

Phototypeset by Input Typesetting Ltd, London
Printed and bound in Great Britain by
Biddles Ltd, Guildford and King's Lynn

British Library Cataloguing in Publication Data
The Principles of riding: the official handbook of the
   German National Equestrian Federation. 2nd ed. – (The
   Complete riding and driving system; bk 1).
   1. Livestock. Horses. Riding
   I. Deutsche Reiterliche Vereinigung II. Series III.
   Grundausbildung fur Reiter und pferd. *English*
   798.23

ISBN 1-872082-01-7

Contents

SECTION TWO
Basic Training of the Horse

Foreword

The German training system is well tried and tested, and their success in all equestrian disciplines proves the point. They have won more championship medals than any other country in the world, including the remarkable achievement of all three team golds at the Seoul Olympic Games.

These achievements must surely stem, in large part, from their basic training methods. Their system, evolved from classical foundations, is logical and progressive with much attention to detail.

It was for these reasons that the British Horse Society Training and Examinations Committee felt that an English translation would be both beneficial and instructive. It is my belief that too many riders have endeavoured to follow too many different routes to achieve their goal. Whilst it is true that 'many roads lead to Rome' it is the chopping and changing of these roads that leads to confusion and delays in arrival.

Contained in this book is one possible road, clearly and positively defined.

Richard Davison

RICHARD DAVISON, FBHS
Chairman, British Horse Society Training and
Examinations Committee

SECTION ONE
Basic Training of the Rider

1. Pre-requisites for the successful training of a rider

1(1) The Instructor

The reasons which motivate people to live and work with horses vary.

Some want to ride solely as a hobby, without ever wishing to compete; some regard it as an alternative way of taking exercise; others want to compete up to the highest level; and in recent times riding for the disabled and therapeutic riding have become more and more popular. For each of these purposes there are many breeds of horses and ponies available.

The instructor's task is to impart to the pupil his knowledge of handling and riding horses in a way that will guarantee good sport, enjoyment and safety. It is therefore obvious that a good instructor must have suitable qualifications as well as many years of experience.

1(2) The Training Centre

It is advisable to start schooling the novice rider indoors. This is the safest method, as a beginner is not able to control the horse, and out of doors the horse is more likely to be distracted by its surroundings. The school should be 20m × 40m. If possible, an outdoor manège should also be available. Ideally one should also have access to an outdoor arena of somewhat larger dimensions, for canter work, practising the forward seat, and jumping. There should be enough material to build a small training course with fences of novice standard. A natural water jump is essential.

The arena is the showpiece of any riding establishment.

A neglected surface, with furrowed or embedded tracks, and fence material carelessly scattered about, is hardly an advertisement for a well-run establishment. Good management, good will, and effort are required to keep the arena neat and tidy, with the surface regularly harrowed and levelled.

Lectures on theory are a necessary supplement for the education of any rider. For this a comfortable lecture room should be available, suitably equipped with blackboard, ciné-screen, projector, wall-charts and whatever teaching aids are necessary to make the subject interesting and comprehensible.

Similarly, practical stable management can only be effectively taught in a stable if suitable equipment is available.

1(3) The Training Programme

At the beginning, a novice rider has to become acquainted with the horse. He should learn the basic seat position on the lunge. Lunge lessons are best for the beginner because the horse remains under the control of the instructor who can then concentrate on developing the rider's security, balance, and seat position – with medium-length stirrups in all three paces.

Though lungeing the novice rider may seem a waste of time, it is quickly rewarded by more rapid progress in later lessons – a safe, secure seat having been established from the very start.

When the beginner has established the basic seat and can independently control the horse, class rides of six to eight pupils of similar standard can be formed.

Within the class ride the instructor may level the standard by changing the more advanced riders on to slightly more challenging horses. The instructor should occasionally ride all school horses to check their way of going, and should re-school them if necessary.

In the class ride a beginner should always ride with stirrups. Only when his seat and confidence have been established will he be told to cross his stirrups and ride part of the lesson without them.

As long as the rider is not able to ride his horse in a rounded outline, side reins may be used.

A demonstration by an experienced rider on a well-schooled horse, or watching a competition, will enhance the beginner's understanding and make him keen to learn.

Vaulting lessons are an ideal way of familiarizing children with horses at an early age. Also, the riding of ponies makes the introductory stages easier for children.

Vaulting teams and pony rides should be a standard feature of every riding club or riding school.

1(4) Dress and Tack

1(4)i THE RIDER'S DRESS

For the first few lessons the rider needs only comfortable jeans, sweater and jodhpur boots, or rubber riding boots with smooth soles and flat heels. Later on it will be necessary to acquire a correct riding outfit. Especially important are well fitting jodhpurs or riding beeches. They must 'give' enough at the knees and have no wrinkles anywhere, as these may cause saddle sores. The legs of the garment must be loose enough to allow freedom of movement at the crotch.

The leg of the boot must fit right up to the (bent) knee. If it is not long enough it may catch under the saddle flap and interfere with the rider's seat and aids. For safety reasons the sole of the boot must be in one piece up to the heel, or the rider's foot might get trapped in the stirrup.

Riding gloves should always be worn. They must fit comfortably, to keep the hands warm, but must not interfere with the rider's feel. Leather gloves, or leather

Riding gloves with
leather reinforcements

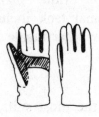

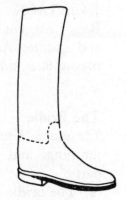

Riding hat, break
(and splinter) proof,
with chin harness

Riding boots
(one-piece sole)

patches on woollen, string or elasticated gloves prevent the reins from slipping.

A suitable hat conforming to the required safety standards must be worn when riding.

To supplement the rather ineffective aids of a beginner, a whip 1 to 1.20 metres (40 to 45 inches) long may be necessary. The whip must not be so flexible that it taps the horse with every movement. But it must be manageable enough to allow the rider to give precise aids with the slightest hand movement. For jumping, a shorter whip of no more than 80cm (30ins) is usual.

It is up to the instructor to decide when a rider's position is established enough to allow spurs. Spurs must fit comfortably, positioned horizontally or tipping slightly downwards. They are normally worn five fingers' width above the heel, but short-legged riders may wear them lower down.

A formal riding jacket is not necessary at the beginning. Later on if a showing or hacking jacket is purchased, the shoulders should allow freedom of movement. It must be short enough so that the rider when mounted does not sit on the hem. Sweaters or shirts must be slim-fitting; otherwise the rider's seat may look distorted and his shoulders may appear rounded.

1(4)ii TACK

Basic tack consists of bridle (snaffle, double or bitless) and saddle. Additional tack includes bandages, boots, breastplate, side reins, martingale and auxiliary reins.

The Bridle

The snaffle bridle is the most suitable for basic training, jumping, and cross-country riding. It consists of two parts:

(a) The bridle itself, with snaffle bit and reins.
(b) The noseband.

The bridle consists of head piece, two cheek pieces, throat lash, and browband. The size of the bridle is adjusted by one or two buckles on one or both cheek pieces. (A buckle on top of the head piece is not advisable, as it may injure the rider.)

The usual bit is an ordinary German snaffle bit. The thicker the bit, the softer is its action on the horse's mouth. Recommended thickness at the snaffle rings is 1.6cm (⅗"). In Germany this thickness has to be used in competition. The snaffle rings should be 7cm (2⅘") in diameter.

The difference between the ordinary snaffle, the eggbutt snaffle and the cheek (Australian) snaffle is as follows:

The ordinary loose-ring snaffle By the free movement of its mouthpiece encourages the horse to champ the bit. With wear, the eyelets in the mouthpiece may develop sharp edges which could injure the horse's lips. To prevent this, use plain rubber bit guards. The *eggbutt snaffle* and the *cheek snaffle* safeguard the horse's lips, but some types allow less movement of the mouthpiece.

The reins, made of leather or webbing, are attached to the bit with buckles or studs and are joined by another buckle. Both reins should be about 2.75m (9ft) long and 2.5cm (1") wide. Web reins, especially when fitted with

Snaffle bridle with drop noseband
1 Head piece
2 Cheek piece
3 Throat lash
4 Browband
5 Headpiece of noseband
6 Nosepiece of noseband
7 Chinstrap of noseband
8 Noseband rings
9 Snaffle bit
10 Reins
11 Martingale stop

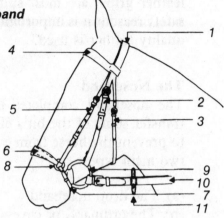

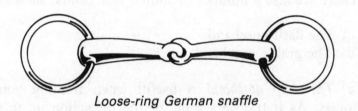

Loose-ring German snaffle

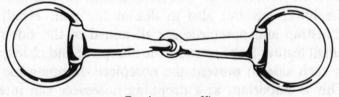

Eggbutt snaffle

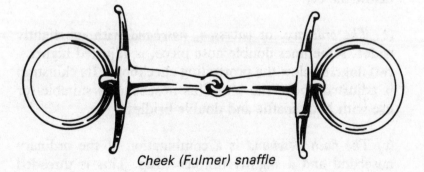

Cheek (Fulmer) snaffle

leather grips, are most suitable for wet conditions. For safety reasons it is important that only well-stitched, good-quality leather is used.

The Noseband

The noseband completes the bridle. Its purpose is to transfer some of the bit's effect on to the nasal bone and to prevent the horse from evading the rein aid. There are two main types:

(a) The drop noseband
(b) The ordinary, or cavesson, noseband.

There are also a number of similar nosebands, such as:

(c) The flash noseband
(d) The grakle noseband.

(*a*) *The drop noseband* is useful when training young horses. As it transfers some of the bit action on to the nasal bone, it prevents the mouth from opening and the jawbone from locking. The horse is thus obliged to submit the lower jaw but also to flex at the poll. Headpiece, chinstrap and nosepiece are all joined to the side-rings. Small leather loops connect the nosepiece and cheekpieces at each side to prevent the nosepiece dropping too low. This is important as a dropping nosepiece can interfere with the horse's breathing. The chinstrap is adjusted below the bit.

(*b*) *The ordinary*, or *cavesson, noseband* with its slightly wider, sometimes double nose piece, is adjusted higher – two fingers below the protruding cheekbone. Its chinstrap is adjusted above the bit. This noseband is suitable for use with both snaffle and double bridles.

(*c*) *The flash noseband* is a combination of the ordinary noseband and a slightly thinner strap. This is threaded

Drop noseband

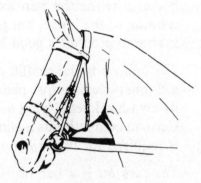

**Ordinary or
cavesson noseband**

Flash noseband

Grakle noseband

through a little loop below the nosepiece of the noseband and is adjusted below the bit.

(*d*) *The grakle noseband* consists of two leather straps, crossing each other on the nasal bone, one chinstrap adjusted above and one below the bit.

The Double Bridle

The double bridle allows an experienced rider on a trained horse to refine the rein aids. It is not used in the basic training of the horse, but is introduced only when a rider is able to produce a good Novice Test in a snaffle bridle.

The bridoon is the snaffle part of the double bridle. It is a thinner-than-normal plain snaffle bit and is attached to its own headpiece, lying under the curb-bit headpiece. In German competitions a minimum thickness of 10mm (⅖″) is required for the bridoon.

The curb bit is a bar bit with two cheeks, whose length and the length of the curb chain determine the force of the bit (lever action). This force is also influenced by the port and the thickness of the mouthpiece. In German competitions a thickness of 16mm (⅗″) measured at the cheeks, is compulsory. The higher the port the more the tongue is fixed into position and the more firmly the sides of the mouthpiece rest on the bars (stronger influence). The cheeks are divided into upper and lower, and their length should have a ratio of 1:1.5 or 1:2.

In dressage competitions in Germany a lower cheek length of 5–10cm (2–4″) is allowed. In all other competitions where a double bridle is permitted, its cheeks may not exceed a length of 7cm (2¾″).

The headstall is attached to the ring at the upper cheek. The curb rein, slightly narrower than the bridoon rein, is attached to the movable ring at the lower cheek. If necessary, a lip strap can be threaded through the fly ring at the centre of the curb chain and attached to the little

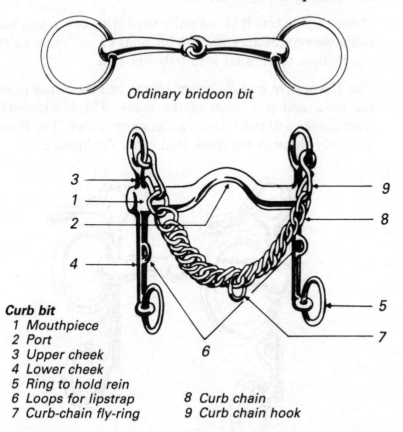

Ordinary bridoon bit

Curb bit
1 Mouthpiece
2 Port
3 Upper cheek
4 Lower cheek
5 Ring to hold rein
6 Loops for lipstrap
7 Curb-chain fly-ring
8 Curb chain
9 Curb chain hook

hole in the centre of each cheek. The lip strap keeps the curb chain in position.

The curb chain is straightened with a right-hand twist and hung from the top by the curb chain hooks. The hooks open upwards and are twisted to the outside. This is important, as distorted hooks may injure the horse's cheeks.

Other specialized bits and bridles
The Pelham, Hackamore, Bosal, etc., should be used under special circumstances only, and under knowledgable supervision.

The Pelham is a snaffle bit with the cheeks and curb chain of the double bit. It is normally used with two reins, but roundings connecting the two bit rings on each side allow the Pelham to be used with only one rein.

The Hackamore and Bosal are bitless bridles acting upon the nasal and jaw bones of the horse. The Hackamore, with cheeks and curb chain, is the more severe. The Bosal acts only through the thick lead rope, the 'mecate'.

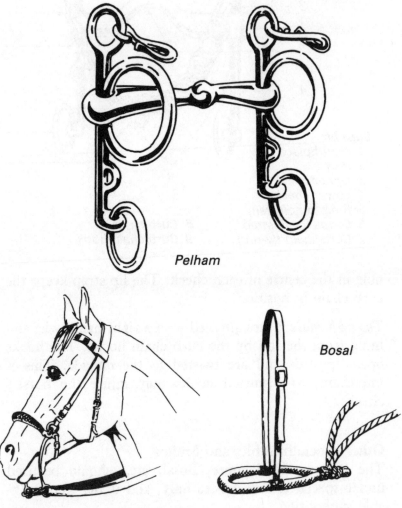

Pelham

Bosal

Hackamore

The Saddle

The parts of the saddle are:

The tree, or skeleton, of the saddle, which determines its shape. It can be made of steel, leather, fibre glass, laminated wood, whale bone, or a combination of materials.

The pommel, the high-curved front of the saddle. It has to be high, so that – especially with the rider's weight in the saddle – it does not touch the withers, where the long dorsal fins of the vertebrae are protected only by skin. The pommel must be not only high but also wide enough to fit the individual horse. The width of the pommel determines the size of the saddle.

The cantle, the back end of the seat.

The stirrup bar, which holds the stirrup leathers. For safety reasons it must be firmly attached to the tree.

The panel contains the padding between the tree and the horse's back. It is made of horse hair or felt, covered with leather. The panel should not be thicker than is absolutely necessary, so that the rider can be as close to the horse as possible.

Knee rolls, the thick padding at the front of the panel. They keep the rider's legs in place.

The seat, which by its shape influences the rider's position. Its deepest point should be at the centre.

The saddle flaps, which by their shape determine whether the saddle is for dressage or jumping. The flaps must be of firm and good quality leather.

The straps, which hold the girths, and for safety reasons should be of top-grade leather, and handstitched. They are fitted with a buckle-guard to protect the flap from the girth buckles.

Parts of the saddle

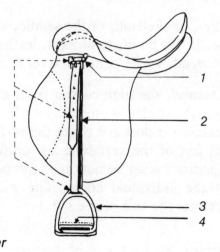

1 Stirrup bar
2 Stirrup leather
3 Stirrup
4 Stirrup tread

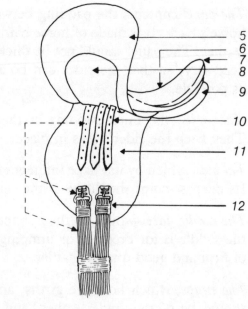

5 Saddle flap
6 Seat
7 Cantle
8 Buckle guard
9 Panel
10 Girth straps
11 Sweat flap
12 String girth with buckles

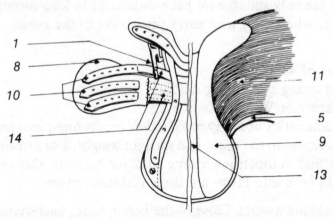

1 *Stirrup bar*	9 *Panel*
5 *Saddle flap*	10 *Girth straps*
8 *Buckle guard*	11 *Sweat flaps*

13 *Gullet*
14 *Pre-strained webbing, stretched and secured across the waist of the saddle tree.*

The girth, which must be wide enough to prevent galling. Forged buckles are better than cast or nickle. Types of girths are: the German wide-web girth (best because it does not wrinkle, lets air through, is inexpensive, and is easy to clean); the leather girth; and the web or synthetic girth.

Stirrup leathers must be of supple, durable leather. The fold-back at the buckle should be at least 7cm (2¾") long, and handstitched. Oval-shaped holes are more practical for easy girth adjustment.

The stirrups must be wide enough (full size 12cm or 4¾"; children 10cm or 4") and heavy so that the rider's foot can easily slide in and out. *Rubber treads* give a firmer grip to the rider's foot. The eyelet of the stirrup must be smooth so as not to wear the stirrup leather unnecessarily.

Numnahs keep the horse's sweat from the saddle padding. They must be easy to wash (a dirty numnah can cause infection) and firm enough not to wrinkle when in use.

They should be shaped, to avoid putting pressure on the withers. Thick, folded blankets used as saddle cloths prevent the rider from being close enough to the horse. They are only suitable for pack-saddles or in long distance riding, where they give extra protection to the horse.

Types of saddle

(a) Sporting or hunting saddle
(b) Army or Western saddle

Characteristics of the *sporting saddle* are its one-piece tree, its closeness to the horse and its light weight. For ordinary sport and competition riding and for hunting this type should be used. There are three different styles:

DRESSAGE SADDLE Close to the horse, long, near-vertical flaps.

JUMPING SADDLE Longer seat, forward-cut flaps with knee rolls.

GENERAL-PURPOSE SADDLE A cross between a dressage and a jumping saddle, and suitable for both purposes. Nowadays it is often used in show jumping.

The *Army* or *Western saddle* has two separate halves to its tree, one on each side of the horse's spine. It is of stronger build and therefore more suitable for weight and pack carrying.

Auxiliary reins

These *may* be used by experienced horsemen when training difficult horses or re-training spoiled horses. If used correctly they should improve the contact and submissiveness of the horse. They also counteract excessive upward head movement.

When using auxiliary reins the trainer must be aware that the same results will have very soon to be achieved without them.

The most common auxiliary reins are:

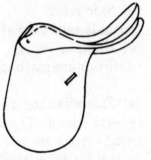

Dressage saddle

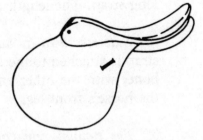

Jumping saddle

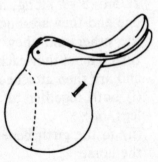

General-purpose saddle

Military saddle

(a) Side reins
(b) Side rein used as a standing martingale
(c) Running reins
(d) Running martingale

(a) *Side reins* are narrow leather straps, 1.20m – 1.50m (4'–4¾') long. Those fitted with rubber rings or elasticated inserts are not recommended. One end is attached to the bit by a buckle or snap hook; the other end is attached to the girth or lungeing roller by a buckle and a long strap. The length of the side rein is adjustable.

(b) *Side rein used as standing martingale* The end of the strap is attached to the cavesson noseband under the jaw-bone, with the other end attached to the girth, between the horse's front legs.

(c) *The running rein* consists of two reins, each 2.50 – 2.75m (8'–9') long, made of plain leather or webbing. At one end they are buckled together like ordinary reins; at the other end they are fitted with buckles. From the rider's hand they each run towards and through a bit ring, and are then attached, either:
(i) both together to the girth between the horse's front legs, or
(ii) to the girth beneath the saddle flap on either side of the horse.

(d) *The ring martingale* or *running martingale* is a leather strap with an adjustable loop at one end, through which the girth is threaded. The martingale comes forward from between the horse's front legs and divides into a fork with a ring at each end. The reins are threaded through the rings. As the rings move loosely on the reins it is necessary to fit stoppers, which prevent the rings from catching on the rein-buckles near the bit.

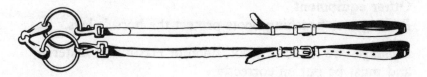

Side reins

Standing martingale

Running reins

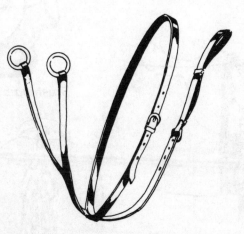

Running martingale

Other equipment

Bandages or brushing boots protect the horse's legs.

Bandages are made of wool, linen or elasticated material, and must be put on correctly.

Brushing boots are made of felt, leather, or padded, synthetic material. They must fit well, shaped around the fetlock joint, they must be easy to wear, and they must not impede the horse's movement.

Horses with low withers need an undergirth, or fore-

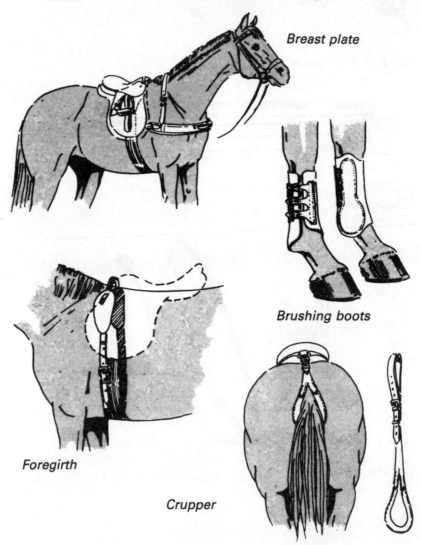

Breast plate

Brushing boots

Foregirth

Crupper

girth. This keeps the saddle from slipping forwards. With ponies and hacking horses a crupper can be used to achieve the same effect.

A breastplate (racing) keeps the saddle from slipping backwards (especially with fit horses).

1(4)iii CARE OF TACK

Good quality tack can be very expensive, but if properly cared for and stored it will last for a long time. This involves:

(a) Cleaning all tack each time it is used.
(b) Preserving leather according to use – weekly or less often.
(c) Carefully and regularly checking all moving parts and stitching.
(d) A 'spring clean' of all tack about twice a year.
(e) Storage of tack.

(a) Daily cleaning after use

Metal parts should be cleaned with water, and dried. While doing this it is important not to wet leather parts, reins, cheekpieces etc.

Leather All sweat and dirt should be removed with a damp sponge. When leather is nearly dry, apply saddle soap.

Saddle cloths should be washed or dried, and brushed according to material. Preferably a clean saddle cloth should be used each day.

Girths must be thoroughly cleaned every day.

(b) Preservation

Leather tack must be completely dismantled before it is thoroughly cleaned. When nearly dry apply either saddle soap or harness oil. Some parts of the tack – e.g. saddle flaps – do not come into contact with the horse and need special attention. To these parts a thin layer of saddle soap should be applied by hand and thoroughly rubbed in (the warmth of the hand helps the soap to penetrate the leather). The parts of the leather which come into contact with the horse (e.g. saddle padding) should be given a thin coating of special leather oil.

Leather needs moisture from saddle soap or leather oil to maintain its suppleness. Oil keeps it flexible, but too much oil softens the consistency of the grain and weakens the leather.

Metal parts should be cleaned and lightly oiled. Bits must never be cleaned with chemicals.

Rubber, plastic and suede should be cleaned with a damp cloth or sponge.

Bandages and *numnahs* must be washed and dried.

(c) Checking Moving Parts and Stitching
Defective stitching should be repaired immediately. Metal parts (e.g. snaffle bits) showing sharp edges, cracks or any signs of metal fatigue, must be replaced.

(d) Spring Cleaning
The dismantled pieces of tack should be thoroughly cleaned with luke warm water and green soap (pure soap), then dried away from artificial heat. Afterwards they may be soaped or oiled as in (b) above.

(e) Storage
Tack should be stored in a dust-free room. Air temperature must be kept constant in all weathers, as extremes of heat, cold or damp will damage harness. Bridles should be hung up. Saddles should be stored on saddle racks, paying particular attention to the saddle tree.

Pieces of equipment not in regular use should be given

a thicker coating of soap or oil and hung up. Occasional airing and wiping prevents moulding.

1(5) Preparing an Arena

1(5)i MARKERS AND TRACKS

To maintain order and uniformity in any riding school it is necessary to adopt standard rules and markers.

For the training and riding of dressage tests in a 20×40m arena, letters are used as markers.

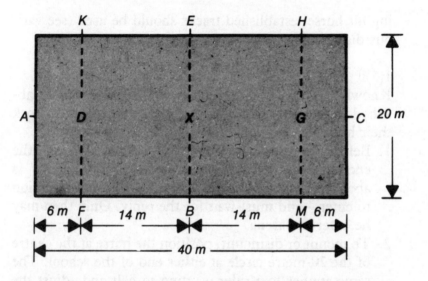

For ordinary riding in a 20×40m arena the following markers (shown on the diagram overleaf) are sufficient: one marker (a short, black straight line is sufficient) at the centre of each long side; four changing points, two on each long side, each 6m (19′ 8″) from the corners; six circle markers (large red dots), one at the centre of each short side, two on each long side, 10m (33ft) from the corners. At these markers the circle touches the track. (There should also be an 'imaginary' circle marker in the centre of the school.)

In the arena, especially if more than one rider is work-

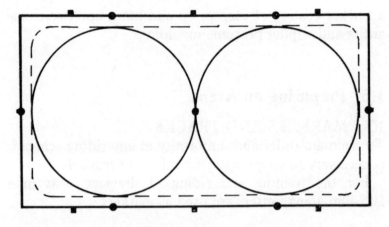

ing his horse, established tracks should be used (see various diagrams).

1(5)ii ARENA ORDER

Knowledge of and compliance with certain well established rules are necessary to enable several riders to work their horses at the same time without interference.

1. Before entering an arena and before opening the enclosure the rider must make sure that nobody is about to pass the exit. Then he has to ask permission to enter – and must wait for the reply. Only then may he enter the arena.
2. To mount or dismount, position the horse at the centre of the 20-metre circle at either end of the school. The same applies to a rider wanting to halt and adjust the girth or stirrups.
3. Always keep a safe distance of 3m (10ft) from other horses.
4. Riders at a walk or giving their horses a rest should use the inside track (2m or 6½ft from wall), leaving the outside track free.
5. Riders on a circle must give way to riders on the track 'going large' (following the outside track of the school).
6. When riders ride on both reins they should always pass each other left leg to left leg.
7. Following a command to change rein – or to ride on

20×40m dressage arena – markers and movements

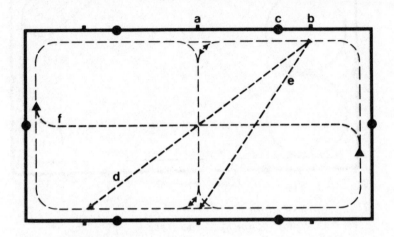

a) Half school marker
b) Changing point
c) Circle marker
d) Changing rein across the diagonal
e) Changing rein across the short diagonal
f) Changing rein down the centre line

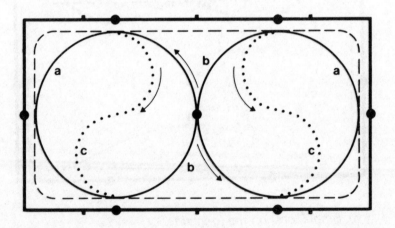

a) Circles
b) Changing out of the circle
c) Changing through the circle

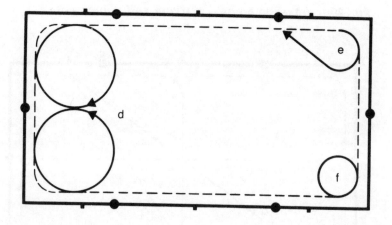

d) Figure of eight
e) Half-volte, inclining to the track
f) Volte

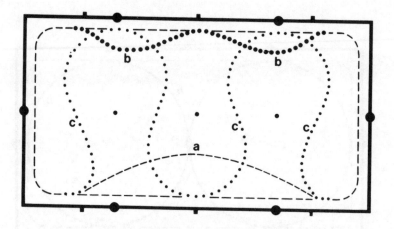

a) Single loop on the long side
b) Double loop on the long side
c) Serpentine (five loops)

a named rein only – riders already on this rein have right of way. Riders who have not yet changed rein must give way and use the inside track.

8. If other riders are present, lungeing a horse in the arena may only be carried out with their permission. It can only be done safely if the lunge horse is well behaved. During a class lesson there should be no lungeing.
9. Only during a jumping training session should there be fence material in the arena. At all other times the school must be completely free – including the corners.

1(6) Preparing the Horse for Riding

1(6)i PUTTING ON THE BRIDLE

Horses in loose boxes must first be caught, tied up with a head collar or fitted with a bridle, and then saddled. Horses in stalls should be first saddled and then bridled.

To tack up, hold the bridle correctly in your left hand. Approach the horse from the left side. Stand alongside his neck, facing forward.

With your right lower arm around the horse's head, and your right hand on his nasal bone, hold the horse without restricting his breathing. When he is standing quietly, slip the reins over his head and neck. Put your right hand on his nasal bone again. Pass the bridle from left hand to right. With the right hand take the two cheek pieces, pulling gently upwards; with the left hand lift the bit up between the horse's lips. Well handled horses will willingly take the bit. Otherwise, the thumb of your left hand should be pushed between his lips just behind the incisors, to encourage him to open his mouth and accept the bit, while pulling the bridle a little higher with the right hand.

The now free left hand can be used to lift the headpiece over the ears. With the right hand push the ears gently forward, one by one. Then fasten the throatlash and noseband.

The same care must be taken when removing the bridle as when putting it on. Unfasten the throatlash and noseband, then standing alongside the horse's neck, take hold of one end of the browband with each hand and push the headpiece forward over the ears. Gently lower the bridle, waiting for the horse to open his mouth and drop the bit. In this way the bit will not touch the teeth and frighten the horse.

The bridle is correctly fitted when the bit lies high enough to touch the corners of the mouth without pulling them up. A bit lying lower or even touching the incisors will cause pain and difficulties.

The headpiece should rest flat, just behind the ears, without chafing the base of the ears. If the headpiece rubs the ears the browband is too short. The throatlash should be adjusted so loosely that a hand held upright will fit between lash and jawbones. The throatlash should hang just below the middle of the cheek bone.

The drop noseband is correctly adjusted when it lies about four fingers above the nostrils. The side-rings of the noseband must lie above the bit, otherwise the noseband is too long. The buckle of the chinstrap, when fastened, must lie on the left side of the lower jawbone, otherwise it will exert pressure on the back of the lower jawbones.

The ordinary or *cavesson noseband* is correctly adjusted when it lies about two fingers below the protruding cheek bone. It may be adjusted tightly enough to allow one finger to fit between noseband and nasal bone. For the buckle of the chinstrap the same applies as for the drop noseband.

Tacking up with a double bridle is the same as for the snaffle bridle. But special care has to be taken in adjusting the bits.

Snaffle bridle with
drop noseband

Double bridle with
cavesson noseband

The bridoon should touch the corners of the mouth but must not pull them up.

The curb bit should lie a little below the bridoon, but not so low that it interferes with the animal's tushes. The width of the curb is important: it must be wide enough to allow about ½cm (⅕″) space on each side. If the bit is wider it will tilt in the mouth and put more pressure on to one of the bars. If it is narrower it will press against the corners of the horse's mouth.

The curb chain should be turned clockwise to make it lie flat in the chin groove, in line with the mouthpiece of the curb. It should be linked into the curb chain hooks so that it maintains its right-hand twist. A surplus link should hang down on the near side. If the extra links form an even number they should be divided equally on each side. If the number of extra links is uneven, the larger number should remain on the near side.

THE LENGTH OF THE CURB CHAIN should be adjusted so that when a contact is taken up with the curb reins the cheeks of the curb and the mouth form an angle of 45°. If the cheeks do not reach this angle but contact is achieved with the cheeks closer to the mouth, the curb

chain is too short. If the angle is more than 45°, the curb
chain is too long.

THE CURB BIT IS THE CORRECT SIZE if the curb chain
does not slide upwards when contact is taken up; the curb
chain hooks must now maintain their position in relation
to the upper cheeks of the curb. If the angle between the
hooks and the upper cheeks increases, the curb chain will
be too short, causing the corners of the mouth to be
pinched and injured.

The links of the curb chain should mould smoothly
around the jawbones, which will only be possible if the
mouthpiece of the curb is the correct width for the horse.

For horses with mouth deformities, or those who try
to snatch or bite at the cheeks of the curb bit, a lip strap
can be of help. This strap is round-stitched and leads
from the D on one cheek through the fly ring on the curb
chain to the D on the other cheek. For horses with sensitive skin it is advisable to use a protective (leather or
rubber) cushion under the curb chain.

1(6)ii PUTTING ON THE SADDLE

Before lifting the saddle on to the horse, check that the
irons are run up, that the girth is attached to the girth
tabs on the off side, and that it is lying across the saddle.

The horse should be approached on the near side. Lift
the saddle on to the withers and then gently push it
backwards – with the hair – into its proper position. A
normal saddle will lie behind the shoulder, giving it freedom of movement, and the deepest point of its seat will
be in the centre.

It is important to adjust the numnah correctly, without
wrinkles. It must be well pulled up into the front arch,
avoiding pressure on the withers. Ensure that the withers
remain free of pressure after the girth has been tightened
and after the rider's weight has been added.

Having put the saddle into position, the rider should
move to the horse's off side and lift down the girth,
checking that numnah and girth tabs are lying correctly.

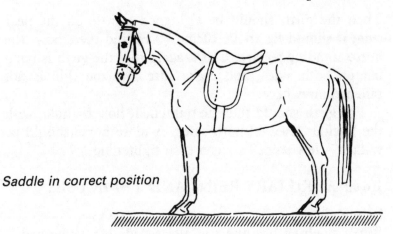

Saddle in correct position

Saddle too far back

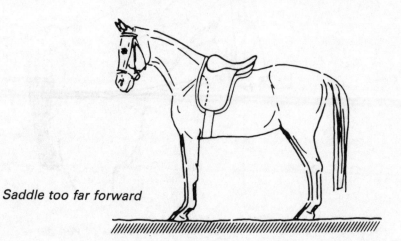

Saddle too far forward

Then the girth should be tightened a little on the near side; it should lie about 10cm (4") behind the elbow, the horse standing square. Check again that the girth is lying flat on both sides, and make sure that the skin is not pinched anywhere.

The girth should then be tightened, hole by hole, with the buckles level on both sides. A tense horse should be walked a few steps between each tightening.

1(6)iii AUXILIARY REINS AND THEIR USES

Side Reins

When teaching beginners in a class ride it may be necessary to tack horses up with side reins. This must be done only with reliable horses. The side reins should be attached to the girth between the buckles on both sides, so that it is impossible for them to slip down. When attached to the bit, the side reins should be in a horizontal position, a little above the point of the shoulder.

Both side reins should be adjusted to equal length and

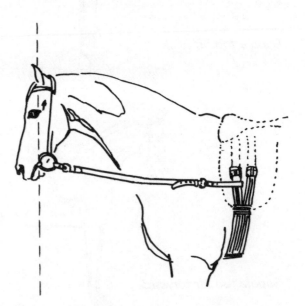

Side reins attached correctly. Nose in front of vertical.

with such contact that the horse's nasal bone is in front of the vertical.

During longer walking sessions, especially at the end of the lesson or when jumping, the side reins *must be undone*. They should then be hooked into the front Ds of the saddle on each side of the withers, taking care that they are not so long as to loop in front of the rider's foot, which would obviously be dangerous.

The standing martingale is one side rein leading from the girth between the horse's front legs to the horse's head, where it is attached to the chinstrap of the noseband. Its length should be adjusted so that the horse's mouth is in a horizontal line with his hip bones.

There are very few cases where the use of a standing martingale is necessary or even advisable. Compared with side reins, the standing martingale offers more sideways freedom for the horse's head and neck. But its disadvantages are that it is very restrictive and that the under-neck muscles are worked more and therefore developed, which is not desirable. The standing martingale thus has a limited value. When having to restrict horses for beginners it may be advisable to use *double side reins*, which are two reins each 2.25m (just over 7ft) long. They should be attached to the girth a little higher than the normal side reins, then threaded through the bit rings from the inside towards the outside and back to the girth, to which they should be attached in the normal side rein position.

Compared with ordinary side reins the double side rein allows a little more elasticity and makes it a little easier for the horse to lower its neck.

The running rein is attached to the girth in the same way as the side rein, or between the front legs like a martingale. It is then threaded through the bit rings and is carried in the rider's hand as a second pair of reins.

The running rein must be used only by an experienced rider who can activate the horse's quarters and who understands the importance of the forward driving aids. It must

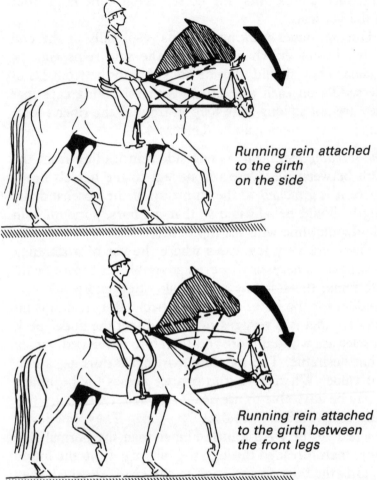

*Running rein attached
to the girth
on the side*

*Running rein attached
to the girth between
the front legs*

be used independently from the reins and yielded as soon as the required effect is achieved. *The running rein can never replace correct training or riding a horse correctly on the bit.*

The running martingale should not be used to tie a horse's head down, but if a horse carries his head unusually high or throws it up it can be of value. If, for instance, when approaching a fence, a horse suddenly throws up its head and tries to evade the aids, the running martingale will

The effect of the running martingale, which prevents a horse from throwing up his head

help the rider to stay in control and will also protect him from being hit in the face by the horse's head.

A martingale is correctly fitted if the straight line of the reins from the bit to the rider's hand is not distorted.

Too short a running martingale has a negative effect similar to that of the tight standing martingale: the constant downward pressure provoking an upward resistance from the horse which in turn encourages the development of (unwanted) under-neck muscles.

1(6)iv LEADING A HORSE IN HAND

When leading a saddled horse, the irons should be run up and secured, with the leathers tucked away. Dangling irons can frighten a horse or get caught on door handles, water taps, etc.

To lead a horse, take the reins over the neck and hold them about 10cm (4″) away from the bit. They should be divided by the index and middle fingers. The rein on the off side should be held a little more tightly than the near one. The end of the reins should also be held in the right hand and secured with the thumb.

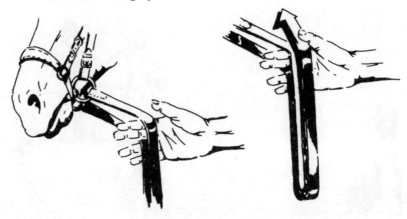

Taking up the reins to lead a horse

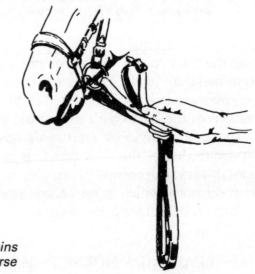

*How to hold the reins
when leading a horse*

□ If the horse is tacked up with a double bridle, the curb reins should remain over his neck.

□ Leading a horse with a head collar may only be safely done in an indoor school or an enclosed yard.

□ When leading an impatient or badly mannered horse, the handler should always be by the horse's shoulder, trying to control him with short, sharp jerks, especially on the right rein. Extra control can be achieved by keeping the left hand over the horse's eye.

*Leading a fresh horse:
raising left hand
in front of the eye*

□ When showing or parading a horse, all turns should be right-hand ones. This makes for better control and also shows the onlooker more of the horse than of the handler.

□ If a lead horse shies or plays about, it is important not to let the reins get longer, as this would be unsafe for the handler, coming within striking range of the horse's quarters.

□ A rearing horse is especially dangerous. To bring him down, try a sideways rein action, avoiding the risk of being struck by the front hooves.

□ Special care has to be taken while leading horses in single file (one following another). A distance of 5m (about 16ft) should be kept between each horse. Pupils have to be constantly reminded of this.

2. The Seat

2(1) Mounting and Dismounting

When mounting or dismouting in the arena the rider should get into the habit of making the horse stand correctly on the centre line. If mounting while other riders are working their horses, the centre of a 20 metre circle should be used.

The horse must learn to stand absolutely still until the rider is ready to move off. There should be complete immobility for at least half a minute. If insisted on every day the horse will have no problems with the first or last halt in a dressage test.

Before mounting, the rider should always have one arm through the reins while pulling down the irons, organising stirrup leathers, and tightening the girth. Never leave the horse standing without holding the reins. This would be grave neglect, as even the quietest horse can become frightened and take off, with disastrous consequences.

First the stirrup leathers have to be adjusted. An approximate measure is your arm length: from fingertips at saddle-bar to armpit at stirrup base. The exact length of the stirrup leathers depends on the length of the rider's legs, the shape of the horse's barrel, and his movement. In the dressage seat position the stirrups should be of such length that the rider can sit with a deep knee, maintaining contact with the inside of his calf muscle. It is wrong to try to achieve this contact by shortening the stirrups, which merely raises the rider's knee and pushes the seat backwards.

Too long a stirrup makes it difficult for the rider to sit still and apply proper leg aids, so that he fails to put enough weight on to his seat bones and rides too much on the fork.

To mount, the rider should stand on the near side, close to the horse's shoulder. He takes up contact with the reins in the left hand, the rein on the off side being slightly shorter than the near one. Should the horse move off, his body would come closer to the mounting rider.

Facing backwards, the rider's left hand, while holding the reins, should also take hold of a tuft of mane close to the withers. With the help of his right hand he places his left foot in the stirrup. Then he reaches across the saddle with his right hand to grip the seat on the off side. Pushing off with his right foot, transferring his weight on to the left stirrup and pulling with the right hand, he mounts and swings his right leg well across the horse's croup. At the same time his right hand is moved to the right knee roll, supporting his weight while he is gently lowering himself into the saddle. Before he settles into the sitting position his weight should first be taken by both thigh muscles. Then he places his right foot quietly in the stirrup and takes up the reins.

If the horse is wearing a *double bridle*, the same routine is followed, but special care is necessary when taking up the reins. The curb reins should be separated by the ring finger; the left bridoon rein should lie under the little finger; and the right bridoon rein should be between the middle and index fingers. All four reins should leave the hand over the second joint of the index finger.

Tightening the girth is best done after walking a while. The rider should take the reins in one hand, lift the leg forward in front of the knee roll – the foot remaining in the stirrup – and with the free hand tighten the girth on that side, hole by hole.

When dismounting, the rider should also make a habit of standing his horse correctly. If dismounting near the stable, the horse should have his back to the building so that he won't be tempted to move towards it.

To dismount, the reins should be held in the left hand,

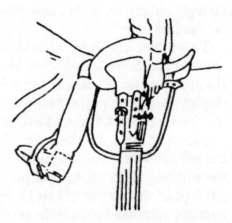

Tightening the girth

and the right hand should be placed on the right knee roll to support the rider's weight. Both feet should be taken out of the stirrups. The rider should then lean forward and swing his right leg over the horse's croup, landing with both feet on the ground.

The stirrups should be run up, and the girth loosened a couple of holes, but not so much that the saddle can slip around the horse.

During and after dismounting, the rider must keep his arm through the reins at all times and must never leave the horse unattended until he is taken back to the stable.

2(2) Seat Positions

The correct seat is the basic prerequisite for the effective application of all aids.

The rider has to achieve an independent balanced seat, without any means of artificial support, tension, gripping up, or stiffness.

His aim should be to follow smoothly the horse's movement, keeping his centre of gravity in harmony with that of the horse. This can only be achieved through intensive tuition and practice. Only the relaxed rider can sit in a secure balance, and only when this is achieved can the trainer start to refine the rider's position.

There are three principal seat positions:
The Dressage Seat
The Light Seat
The Forward (or Jumping) Seat
The transition from one seat position to another must be fluent.

2(2)i THE DRESSAGE SEAT

The dressage seat is the *basic* seat. It is used when training a horse and rider for dressage and in executing dressage movements. When teaching a beginner careful attention should be paid to this position.

The foundation of the seat has three points: the two seat bones and the crotch. The rider's seat should rest with muscles relaxed across the saddle. The thighs should lie flat against the saddle and should be turned inwards so that the knee is flat along the saddle. The thighs should be as vertical as is possible without lifting the weight off the seat bones. This will ensure the important deep knee position, which enables the rider to sit deeper in the saddle and closer to the horse, embracing the horse's barrel.

Turning the knee out is a serious fault. Daylight showing between knee and saddle automatically makes the seat insecure.

On the other hand, when the thigh is turned inwards too much, the knee presses against the saddle. The necessary relaxation is thus impossible, and the rider's lower legs are no longer able to feel the horse or to give effective leg aids.

From below the knee, the rider's legs – depending on their length – should slope backwards/downwards, the flat calf muscles keeping a soft contact with the horse's side. The toes should point forwards and only very slightly outwards.

The stirrup should be positioned under the ball of the foot. The rider's weight should be placed on to the stirrup, passing into the heel. The ankle joint should be supple, flexing freely with the horse's movement, causing the heel to sink below the level of the toe. If the weight is other than evenly placed in the stirrup, the emphasis should be on the inside. Tense inward turning of the toe is as faulty as turning it outwards, or fixing the heel in an exaggerated deep position.

The *upper body* should be positioned vertically above the seat bones, which should be level and square. A common fault is to 'collapse' one or the other hip.

The *back* should be held erect, with the muscles moderately firm to enable them to swing in harmony with the movement of the horse's back. Hollowing the back causes a stiff and tense seat and impairs the rider's influence on the horse.

The *shoulders* should fall naturally backwards from the inhaling chest, producing an imaginary perpendicular line from shoulder to heel.

The *head* should be carried erect – without pushing the chin forward, looking ahead in the direction in which one is riding.

The *upper arms* should hang freely from the shoulder, without being pressed against the sides. Elbows pressed against the body result in pulled-up shoulders and fixed hands and wrist joints. Stiff, stuck-out elbows hinder the seat and the sensitive guidance of the horse.

The *hands* should be closed, with thumbs uppermost, and held vertically.

Every single joint in the rider's body must be relaxed to allow the rider to sit in a supple position and in balance with the horse. Only then can the aids be applied effectively.

2(2)ii THE LIGHT SEAT

The light seat is widely used. It enables a rider to change quickly to the dressage seat or the jumping seat. Therefore it is especially useful for flat work with show jumpers, and in gymnastic jumping when there are frequent changes between flat work and jumping.

It is also a useful seat when hacking or riding across

country, as it combines the advantages of security with lightness. The rider can stay in balance with the horse over uneven terrain and still be light on his back.

The light seat is also of great value when breaking and training young horses. The back muscles of a young horse need strengthening (through gymnastic exercises) before he can carry the full weight of the rider with ease.

As the purpose of this seat is to lighten the burden of the rider's weight on the horse's back, the stirrups should be worn two holes shorter than for the dressage seat. The rider should lean his upper body slightly forward, thus lessening the pressure of the seat bones in the saddle. More of the rider's weight should be carried by his thighs and knees.

His seat, however, should not leave the saddle, and it is important that his lower legs should not slip backwards. His pelvis must follow the horse's movement with suppleness, and all the joints (hip, knee and ankle) must move like a spring to absorb his weight with every stride.

The light seat has to be independently balanced, with hands held still and free of the neck. The reins, the back of the hand, and the lower arm should form one straight line.

At any time the rider must be able to return quickly to the dressage seat.

2(2)iii THE FORWARD (JUMPING) SEAT

Only when the rider has acquired a safe, balanced dressage and light seat can the forward seat be developed. Its purpose is to give freedom to the horse's back and to enable the rider to follow swiftly all changes of the horse's balance, while retaining most of the aid-giving influences of the dressage seat.

This seat should therefore be practised only on horses which have learned to obey the aids in their dressage training.

It is necessary to master the forward seat when show jumping or galloping horses.

Dressage seat

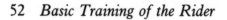

Light seat

Forward (or jumping) seat

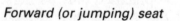

In jumping, it is most obvious over a fence. Between fences the rider will probably change to the light seat.

In order to learn how to apply the aids with short stirrups, you must first practise at the walk and the trot.

The stirrups should be worn considerably shorter than for the dressage seat, depending on the individual physique of the rider. A jumping or multi-purpose saddle should be used, because its knee roll will help to keep the knee steady. The foot may be pushed slightly further into the stirrup to ensure firmer contact of the lower leg. Pushing the foot all the way into the stirrup is not correct, as it immobilizes the ankle joint.

When cantering in forward seat the forward driving aid should be applied by the calf, which should be in steady contact with the horse's side. A lower leg which is sliding backward and forwards inhibits this movement.

The rider's upper body should be positioned in front of the vertical. With 'elastic' hip and knee joints, the seat should be lifted slightly out of the saddle so that it is no longer in but close to the saddle. In this position the seat bones bear no weight. The rider should push his hips well forward while holding his head erect. If necessary he can sit into the saddle to use his weight as an additional forward driving aid.

The important points of the forward seat are the deep heel and knee positions, as well as quiet, steady hands, held low on both sides of the withers. The horse has to canter into the rider's hands, which keep a soft but steady contact. Relaxed shoulder-, elbow- and wrist-joints ensure that the rider's body movements are not transmitted into his hands. They should be completely independent of his seat. An independent and effective forward seat can only be acquired through practice.

A lot of work in forward seat on a comfortable horse will give a young rider the chance to develop the balance and endurance necessary for jumping and riding across country.

In forward seat the rider has to master turns and circles,

as well as changes of speed, over any terrain, including jumps. When riding turns, it is especially important to have a steady contact with the outside rein, so as not to let the horse fall out on to the outside shoulder.

As the name indicates, this seat is primarily used in showing jumping or in training show jumpers. In show jumping, the forward seat is most obvious over a fence. Between fences, the seat will probably change to the light seat.

Only after long and thorough training will a rider be able automatically to adapt his seat to different horses' movements and bounciness. But the work will eventually be rewarded, as only someone with a perfectly balanced independent forward seat, in full control of his body, will be able to adjust to every change of balance and be guaranteed constant success in show jumping. Anything else will remain patchy, and will not give the pleasure which is derived from mastering show jumping.

The forward seat is equally important when taking part in cross-country events. Since different muscles are used in this seat from those used in the dressage seat, they have to be developed by training. If the rider neglects this and gets tired during the steeplechase or cross-country phases, he will put too much weight on to the horse's back, thus placing an unnecessary burden upon the canter movement.

2(3) Incorrect Seat Positions

Tension

Tension is the most common fault in the rider, either throughout or in one part of his body. It makes the seat insecure, causing a lot of unnecessary body movement and diminishing the rider's influence over his horse.

Chair Seat

The rider's weight is not balanced over his heels: instead he sits back in the saddle. Thighs and knees grip up, and the lower leg is much too far forward. In this position the rider cannot apply the aids correctly and therefore lacks control.

Split Seat

In this position the rider transfers too much weight on to the thighs and too little on to the seat bones. The lower legs slip too far backwards. There is thus no secure foundation for a balanced seat.

The cause of most seat faults is the rider's failure to relax. Therefore the first thing that a rider has to learn is a completely relaxed seat. Only when he has achieved this can he be taught position.

The individual position depends on the rider's physique and on the horse's conformation. Any irregularities in the rider's figure (hollow or rounded back, rounded and heavy thighs, weak tummy muscles, etc) can be improved upon or even eliminated by specialized gymnastic training.

In the light or forward seat the most common faults are to go either too little or too much with the movement; or a lower leg which moves too much or is in the wrong position.

It is important therefore that the rider's lower leg (with deep supple knee and ankle joint) should have a firm contact with the horse's side – approximately the same leg position as for the dressage seat, except that the much shorter stirrup necessitates a more acute angle in the knee.

Standing too straight in the stirrups – especially when jumping – or leaning forward to one side of the horse's neck, are just as bad as not getting out of the saddle at all, or even pulling backwards with the hands.

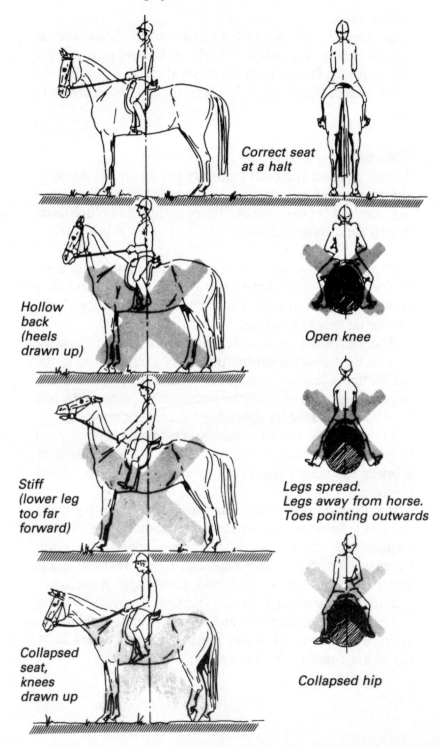

Correct seat
at a halt

Hollow
back
(heels
drawn up)

Open knee

Stiff
(lower leg
too far
forward)

Legs spread.
Legs away from horse.
Toes pointing outwards

Collapsed
seat,
knees
drawn up

Collapsed hip

Causes of Incorrect Seat Positions
RIDER AHEAD OF MOVEMENT
Stirrups too long.
Lower leg too far back.
Heel drawn up.

RIDER TOO HIGH ABOVE THE HORSE
Seat too far away from the saddle.
Heel drawn up.

RIDER BEHIND THE MOVEMENT
Upper body too far back.
Lower leg too far forward.
High hand position, acting backwards.

2(4) Gymnastic Exercises

These are designed to give a rider a safe, relaxed seat, independent of the reins. They should also be used to correct faulty seat positions.

The beginner first learns these exercises at a halt, with the horse tacked up with side reins and held by a responsible person. Later, the pupil may carry out the exercises on the lunge.

On very quiet horses, the exercises may also be practised during a class ride. The reins have to be knotted so short and evenly that the rider can, if necessary, take up immediate contact with the horse. The leading file rider keeps the reins in both hands, the other horses following closely, head to tail. The exercises should not be prolonged. They should be practised first at a walk, then at a trot and also in slow canter. When riding without stirrups it is advisable to remove them from the saddle and to tack the horse up with side reins.

When lungeing a rider to improve his position it is important to use a correct dressage saddle with long flaps.

The following are suggestions for improving a rider's seat position:

Rotating arms, forward, sideways and backwards.

Stretching arms sideways, or folding them behind the head while swivelling the upper body sideways.

Growing tall while sitting in the saddle, stretching both arms sideways/upwards.

Bending upper body forwards/backwards, while stretching arms downwards/upwards (see drawing below).

Bending upper body forwards/downwards.

Gripping both knees together.

Stretching legs far backwards.

Stretching upper body, bending it slightly backwards.

Rotating arms while stretching upper body upwards.

Stretching one leg sideways, lifting it sideways away from the horse's side.

Bending upper body forward with a slightly hollow back.

Relaxed arm rotation.

Rotating arms and bending upper body

3. The Aids

The rider influences his horse by giving aids with his weight, legs, and hands.

The weight aids are the most essential and most influential ones but also the most subtle and least noticeable. They are of particular importance, as the rider's legs can only create the necessary impulsion when supported by the weight aid.

The forward driving aids of weight and legs are always more important than the regulating aids of the reins.

The co-ordination of the various aids controls the horse's posture, the quality of the paces and his overall obedience.

The intensity of the aids is determined by the horse's sensitivity, his stage of training and the purpose for which the aids are given.

To start with, the aids should always be applied gently and then, if necessary to apply strong aids, the rider must afterwards immediately return to more delicate aids in order to keep the horse sensitive. Rough aids make a horse insensitive and spoil him.

The rider's feel and tact are shown by his ability to time and co-ordinate the various aids correctly and to apply them with the appropriate intensity.

While advancing in his training, the rider must be able to apply the aids so that they become less and less noticeable, until finally he seems to control the horse merely with his thoughts and without any visible aids.

Position for forward
driving leg aids

Position for supporting or
forward/sideways
driving leg aids

3(1) The Leg Aids

The horse's absolute obedience to the leg aids is the pre-
condition of the successful training of the horse. Only the
rider whose legs cause the horse's hind legs to reach
actively further forward can eliminate any sideways deviation: therefore only that rider will be able to straighten
his horse and create impulsion. The rider's legs direct and
control the quarters; the horse seems to move between
them as if between two barriers.

The leg aid can only be effective when applied at the
precise moment that the hind foot is leaving the ground.

The forward driving leg aid is applied close behind the
girth (approximately the width of a hand). If the leg aid
is applied further behind the girth it has one of two
effects, depending on the intensity of the aid:

The supporting leg aid, which stops the hind leg from
deviating on the side where the aid is given, or

The forward/sideways driving leg aid, which is applied more
strongly. It causes the hind leg on that side to move
forward sideways away from the leg giving the aid.

3(2) Holding the Reins

Before learning about the rein aids it is necessary to understand how to hold the reins.

3(2)i HOLDING THE REINS WHEN RIDING WITH A SNAFFLE BRIDLE

□ The snaffle reins should pass in equal lengths, and without being twisted, between the ring finger and the little finger of each hand. The ends of the reins should leave the hand over the second joint of the index finger and rest on the horse's off side, underneath the right rein.

□ The rider's hands should be closed. The reins should be prevented from slipping through the hand by pressing with a moderately bent thumb against the second joint of the index finger – not by gripping tightly with the ring finger or by tensing the fist.

□ The hands should be held vertically, thumbs up, to 'frame' the horse's neck with the reins. They should be carried at an equal height and a few inches apart. The actual height of the hands depends on the horse's posture. When looked at from the side, the lower arms and reins should be in a straight line *and the wrist joints must be supple*. A common fault is a half-open hand which causes the rider to slip the reins and draw back his hands close to his stomach.

□ It is very important to remember that the right hand

Correct
Closed hand

Incorrect
Open hand

Holding the snaffle reins

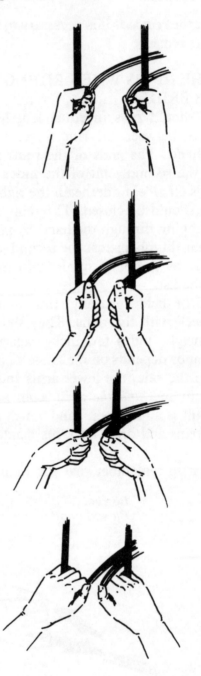

*Correct
hand position*

Incorrect
*Tense,
hollow wrists*

Incorrect
*Tense,
turned-in
wrists*

Incorrect
*Hands
facing
downwards*

should always stay on the right side of the mane, and the left hand on the left side. Crossing the hand over the mane shifts the rider's weight to the wrong side and also causes an incorrect rein aid. This is a dangerous mistake, which should be eradicated right from the beginning.

□ When riding turns and circles, the outside hand should always be carried very close to the neck or withers, so that the rein lies against the neck.

If one rein should have to be held higher than the other – which can be necessary when re-training spoiled horses – this must never be the outside rein when riding on a circle.

3(2)ii HOLDING THE REINS WHEN RIDING WITH A DOUBLE BRIDLE

When riding with a double bridle the reins may be held in various ways. Two reins may be held in each hand (2:2). Alternatively, the left hand may hold both curb reins and one bridoon rein, with the right hand holding the other bridoon rein (this is called the 3:1 rein hold).

(A)   The most common way in which to carry the reins is to hold a curb rein and a bridoon rein in each hand, with the curb rein between the ring and little finger and the bridoon rein below the little finger. The reins should leave the hand together over the index finger and hang down on the off side of the horse's neck. They should, of course, hang between the neck and the right rein.

When holding the reins in one hand (for the salute, etc) the left hand should take the two reins from the right hand, separating them with the middle finger. All rein-ends should hang down on the off side under the right-hand reins.

(B)   This is the same as A, except that the bridoon rein should be held above the curb rein, each being separated by the little finger.

(C)   When riding 3:1, three reins should be held in the left hand and one rein in the right hand. The ring

A

A curb rein and a bridoon rein are held in each hand

B

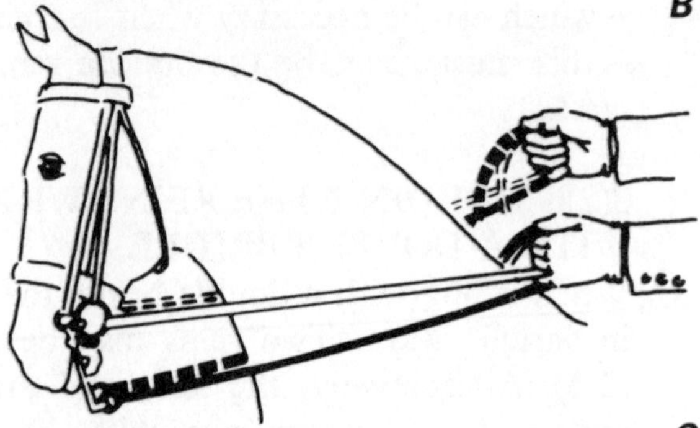

As (A) but with the bridoon rein held above the curb rein

C

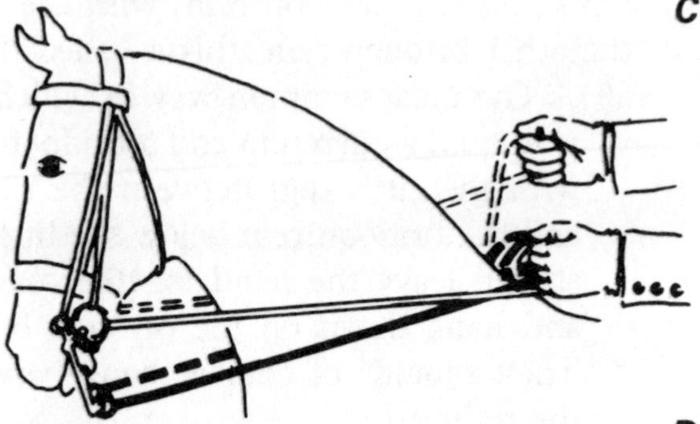

When riding 3:1, three reins are held in the left hand, one rein in the right hand

D

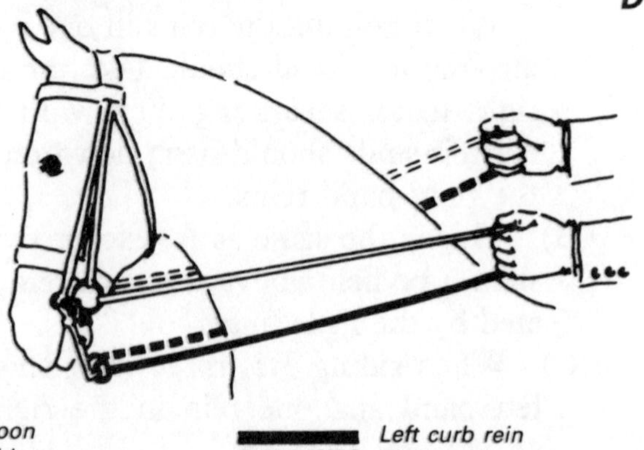

As (B) two reins are held in each hand, but the bridoon rein is held the other way round

――――― Left bridoon	▬▬▬▬ Left curb rein
====== Right bridoon	■ ■ ■ ■ ■ ■ Right curb rein

finger of the left hand should separate the two curb reins, with the right curb rein above the left one. The left bridoon rein should be held below the little finger. The right bridoon rein should be held in the right hand between the ring and little finger. So that the left bridoon rein is the same length as the left curb rein, the right hand should take the left bridoon rein (using the thumb and the first three fingers) and pull it through the left hand until tight enough. Then the right bridoon rein should be picked up with the right hand and held as tightly as the right curb rein. When riding 3:1, the left hand should be carried centrally above the horse's withers. The right hand is carried equally high, the width of two fingers further to the right. The rein ends should be as in (A).

(D)   Two reins are held in each hand, similar to (B), but in this case the bridoon rein is carried the other way round – that is, entering the hand over the index finger.

This method is only for advanced riders when training. It is not desirable in competition.

(E)   When riding with one hand, both curb reins and the left bridoon rein are carried as in (C). The right bridoon rein is fed into the left hand between the index and middle fingers. All four reins leave the hand over the second joint of the index finger and are held in position by the thumb. The rider's right arm extends

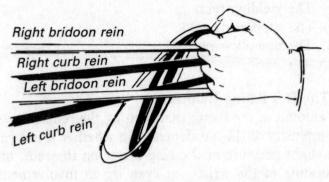

Right bridoon rein

Right curb rein

Left bridoon rein

Left curb rein

Holding the reins with one hand

down naturally from the shoulder, with the hand relaxed and open behind the right thigh, and with the palm facing the horse's rib cage.

Whichever method of holding the reins is adopted, it is essential that the bridoon and curb rein should be held and used independently of each other. Because the curb is a solid bit it is important to give with the outside curb rein in turns, so as not to hurt the horse by putting too much pressure on the outside bars. However, because the bridoon is a jointed bit, the outside bridoon rein can maintain its elastic contact.

Methods (A) and (B) are fairly safe if a pupil is taught from the beginning to be careful.

3(3) The Rein Aids

The rein aids are applied by increasing and decreasing the tension of the reins. *As they are primarily of a regulating nature they must be accompanied by forward driving aids.*

They work more quickly and more effectively if the horse is supple, enabling their influence to flow through the poll and neck, and back into the quarters. *Only the completely supple horse will obey the rein aids willingly.* The rein aids fall into the following categories:

(a) The regulating rein.
(b) The yielding rein.
(c) The supporting rein.
(d) The non-allowing rein.

(a) The Regulating Rein Aid

The amount of regulating achieved by the reins can vary. The intensity of the aid depends on whether it is exerted by a slight pressure of the ring finger on the rein, or by a rounding of the wrists, or even by an involvement of the whole arm. Regulating rein aids are employed in conjunction with the weight and leg aids to achieve the following:

□ To make a downward transition.
□ To shorten the stride within a pace.
□ To halt or rein back.
□ To flex the horse.
□ To make the horse alert.

If the regulating rein aid were to be used on its own to slow down the horse, the horse would 'put on the brakes' with his front legs and fall on to his forehand.

The horse should feel the bit more strongly only because the legs push him on to it more forcefully. It is the legs which must compel obedience in the hand. Therefore, to slow down in balance, the horse has to increase the engagement of the quarters by bringing his hind legs more underneath his body, closer to his centre of gravity.

This can only be achieved if the regulating rein aid is applied in conjunction with the corresponding amount of forward driving aids – the emphasis being on a tightening of the rider's back and seat muscles, which will give his position the necessary stability.

With the regulating rein aid a stern warning has to be given to the rider – never 'get stuck in it.'
Every regulating rein aid must end with a yielding of the reins.

The regulating rein aid must not end up as a 'pulling' on the reins. A prolonged pull on the reins would only cause the horse to lean on the bit rather than to yield to the rein aid.

If the regulating rein aid is not successful immediately, the rider should yield and then repeat the aid in conjunction with the appropriate forward driving aids. This may be done as often as necessary provided each application of the regulating rein aid alternates with a yielding of the reins.

With young or stiff horses, when turning, it may be

necessary on applying the regulating rein aid to move the inside hand sideways, away from the horse's neck towards the rider's inside hip. This, however, must immediately be followed by an exaggerated yielding of the reins – in the direction of the horse's mouth.

(b) The Yielding Rein Aid

This aid can vary in extent from a relaxing of the joints of the fingers to a stretching forward of the whole rider's arm.

The yielding of the rein must not be jerky, as it would cause an interruption in the rhythm of the horse's movement. The contact between hand and mouth should in general be maintained while yielding the rein.

If with the yielding rein aid the rider wants to allow the horse to lengthen his neck, then a yielding of the whole arm is necessary. If more lengthening of the neck is required, the reins may be allowed to slip through the fingers a little while still maintaining contact. To encourage a reluctant horse to lengthen and lower the neck it may be necessary to drop the reins altogether.

(c) The Supporting Rein Aid

The supporting rein aid is given with the outside rein when the horse is bent. The hand applying this rein aid moves close to the neck, but must never cross the mane.

The degree of bend, which is created by inside rein, leg, and weight aids, is controlled by the outside rein.

The amount of support which this rein has to give must be well balanced with the intensity of the inside rein aid. If the outside rein is too strong it prevents the horse from flexing or bending correctly. If it does not support enough, or if the contact is lost altogether, the horse will fall out on to the outside shoulder.

The support given by the outside rein is important. While maintaining a definite contact it usually allows as much as the inside rein needs to create the bend.

Like all other rein aids, this one is also applied in conjunction with a leg aid – the supporting leg aid – which should be applied further behind the girth.

(d) The Non-Allowing Rein Aid

This rein aid *contains* the energy and forward movement which the rider created in the horse with seat, weight and strong forward driving leg aids. The rein aid is sustained with increasing forward driving aids, until the horse submits to it and becomes light in the hand. The forward driving aids must be emphasized. Without them, or if they are too weak, the non-allowing rein aid would be a mere pull.

When using the non-allowing rein aid it is of crucial importance for the rider's hands to *yield* the reins at the exact moment when the horse becomes light, on the bit, and submits in the poll.

When riding on turns and circles, this yielding is of particular significance in relation to the inside rein. Only a horse which is absolutely obedient to the leg aids and therefore going into the bit will willingly obey the rein aids. The rein contact may not be achieved by working backwards with the hands, but must be created by the drive from the quarters which moves the horse's body via a supple back forward into the bit.

In relation to *all* rein aids one has to be constantly reminded of the negative tendency of most riders to do too much with the reins and too little with legs and weight.

The hand only determines the 'frame' within which the horse should move. *The hand should never 'place the head'*, forcing the horse's head and neck into a certain position.

(a) A horse is *on the bit*, when it is submitting to the rider's hands, is supple in the poll, and arching its neck willingly – giving the rider, when moving as well as when at a halt, the feeling of a safe contact between hand and leg.

(b) A horse is *lying on the bit* when it is seeking support from the rider's hands.

(c) A horse is *behind the bit* when it evades the contact between hand and mouth by moving its head backwards and dropping behind the rider's aids.

(d) A horse is *going above the bit* when it tries to avoid submitting to the reins by resisting against the bit with a stiff poll and tensing its neck muscles.

(e) A horse is moving *on a long rein* when the reins are long and the contact light. The horse is not 'on the bit'.

(f) When riding *on a loose rein* the reins are carried so long that there is no contact between rider's hand and horse's mouth.

(g) To test whether or not the horse, when moving freely forward, is carrying himself in balance, one may occasionally *give and retake the reins*. In this exercise the rider's hands move slowly forward along the mane, giving up the contact for a moment. Then the hands return, taking up the contact gently. During this exercise the horse should not lose its balance or increase the tempo.

(h) *Allowing the horse to take more rein.* In this exercise the contact, even on a long rein, is maintained. An opening of the fingers makes the contact lighter, and the horse should follow this by moving his head forward and slightly downwards, gently easing the reins out of the rider's hands. The rider terminates the movement by closing his hands a little more firmly. Afterwards, the rider can either drop the reins altogether, or shorten them again to their normal length.

In this exercise the forward driving leg aids are also of great importance. Allowing the horse to take the reins and lower his head, while maintaining the same rhythm and impulsion, will show the rider if his horse is relaxed and in balance.

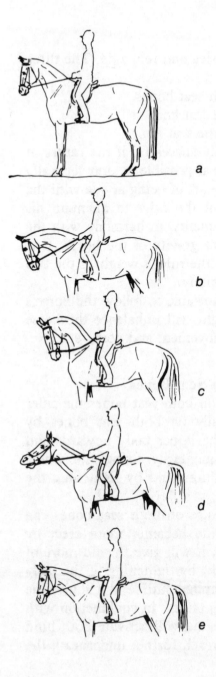

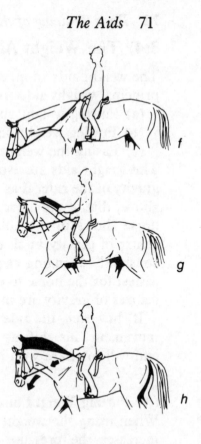

a) The horse is on the bit
b) The horse is
lying on the bit
c) The horse is behind
the bit
d) The horse is going above the bit
e) The horse is moving
on a long rein
f) The horse is
on a loose rein
g) The rider
'gives and retakes'
the reins
h) The rider allows
the horse to take
more rein

3(4) The Weight Aids

The weight aids support the leg and rein aids. The three principal weight aids are:
  (a) Putting weight on both seat bones.
  (b) Putting weight on one seat bone.
  (c) Easing the weight on the seat bones.
The weight aids are especially successful if the centre of gravity of the rider is as close as possible to, and vertically above, that of the horse. The art of being at one with the horse shows in the ability of the rider to maintain his centre of gravity in all movements, in harmony with the constantly changing centre of gravity of the horse. It is easiest for the horse to carry the rider's weight if the two centres of gravity are in harmony.

If, however, the rider is not able to follow the horse's movement, his shifting weight will unbalance the horse and will interfere with his movement and posture.

(A) Putting Weight on Both Seat Bones

When using the weight aid on both seat bones the rider increases the pressure equally on both seat bones by 'growing tall' – stretching the upper body upwards and fractionally backwards, momentarily fixing the whole spine into a more erect position, and by tightening the seat muscles.

The increased equal pressure on both seat bones can have two effects. If the spine becomes more erect by tightening the back muscles, it will give the aid more of a *collecting* effect. If the back, by tightening of the belly muscles, adopts a slightly rounded outline, it will give the aid more of a *forward driving* effect. In conjunction with forward driving leg aids this aid will activate both hind legs and will cause them to reach further underneath the horse's body.

It should therefore be used to support the other aids when increasing the horse's impulsion as well as when collecting the horse.

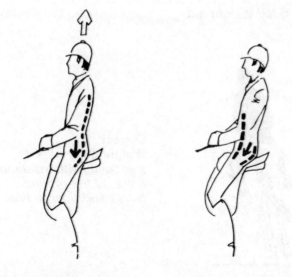

Collecting effect	Forward driving effect

It is a fault to lean back too obviously with the upper body. Also, it is wrong to grip up with the knees and thighs, as it eliminates the forward driving ability of the lower legs.

(B) Putting Weight on One Seat Bone

When using this weight aid the rider shifts his weight noticeably on to one seat bone. This will lower his hip and knee on that side.

Transferring the weight to the left or right seat bone gives the horse the impulse to turn to that side. When turning or bending the horse laterally, the 'one-sided' weight aid is a necessary supplement to the leg and rein aids.

With a schooled horse, the weight aid becomes so predominant that it gives the main impulse for the turn.

It is a fault to collapse a hip. This happens when a rider misunderstands the weight aid, leans inwards too much with his upper body, and pushes his seat to the outside, while gripping up with the inside leg. To prevent this, when using the one-sided (inside) weight aid the rider

The one-sided weight aid

Correct
Weight on the inside seatbone, with inside foot lower to the ground. Horse and rider in line.

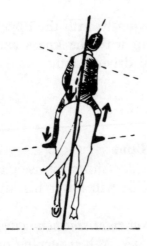

Incorrect
Rider collapses the inside hip. Weight is heavy on outside seat bone. Inside leg is pulled up. Outside heel is closer to the ground than inside one. Inside shoulder is dropped.

should try to push the inside stirrup down to the ground. In this way he will achieve the weight aid correctly.

When riding on turns or circles, or whenever the horse is bent laterally, it is important for the rider's shoulders to be parallel with the horse's shoulders at all times and for the rider's hips to be parallel with the horse's hips.

Therefore, when applying the one-sided weight aid, the rider should move his upper body above the hips in the direction into which he is turning, thus keeping his shoul-

Correct Seat in Turn

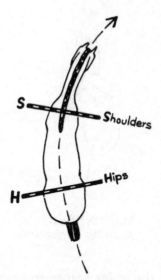

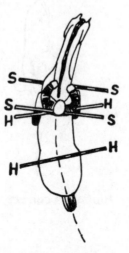

Angle of horse's shoulders
and hips in a turn

Rider's shoulders are
parallel to horse's
shoulders, and rider's
hips are parallel
to horse's hips

ders parallel with the horse's shoulders. This allows the one-sided weight aid to be also a rein aid for a turn. When turning his shoulders, the rider's arms and hands automatically follow suit. The turning of the shoulders gives the inside hand a sideways/backwards effect and the outside hand a sideways/forward effect.

It is a fault to leave the outside shoulder and/or the inside hip behind, as this causes a wrong displacement of the rider's weight and interferes with the flow of the horse's movement.

(C) Easing the Weight on the Seat Bones
When easing the weight in the saddle the rider should transfer his weight equally on to both thighs and on to the stirrups. The seat should remain in the saddle.

Hipbones **correct**　　　**Incorrect** Seat
slipping backwards

Depending on how much the rider wants to ease his weight in the saddle, his upper body should be brought slightly more in front of the vertical.

However, this slight leaning forward is a fault if the hips and seat are not also brought forward. The seat must not be allowed to slip backwards.

3(5) Co-ordination of the Aids

Only by correct co-ordination of the various leg, rein and weight aids can safe control of the horse be achieved. It is not the strength of a rider, but the tactful use of the aids which guarantees success.

A rider has *feel* when he demonstrates the ability to co-ordinate the aids, at the right time, in the correct place, and with suitable intensity. Only a rider who sits relaxed, supple and balanced, constantly in harmony with the horse's movement, can have such feel. When relaxed, the rider is in full control of his own body and can apply the aids with correct intensity independent of the horse's movement.

It cannot be overemphasized that *only a relaxed rider sitting correctly can apply the aids efficiently*.

A soft but effective seat is dependent on the correct position of the rider's spine. On the one hand it must be supple enough to absorb the movement of the horse. On the other hand it must maintain sufficient stability to transmit the rider's aids effectively. (The horse's spine too, must have sufficient suppleness and strength to assure him of the unhindered freedom of his limbs.)

The rider's spine gives firmness to his seat and also acts as a 'central control' from which all aids are transmitted and all the horse's reactions are received.

A correct seat of itself acts as a positive influence on the horse's movement and posture, because the relaxed elasticity of the rider's spine, together with a deep seat and soft embracing leg contact, are stimulating the horse's back movement and impulsion. The rider seems literally to 'sit the horse on to the bit', creating and maintaining his desire for free forward movement. Thus the rider is able to control the horse and to keep the elastic 'spring' in all paces, even in collection.

From the relaxed, embracing rider's legs the horse actually seeks for himself the aid for lively forward movement. The rider's legs 'fall' alternately against the horse's side in rhythm with the pace. This happens because the horse's body is swaying rhythmically and comes into closer contact with the rider's right or left leg when the hind leg on the same side leaves the ground.

When a rider has developed the seat as described, it is easily recognised for its *artistic and aesthetic beauty*.

3(6) Auxiliary Aids

Spurs and whips are used to emphasise the forward driving aids. (In some cases – but only by experienced riders – they may be used to punish a horse.) The voice is also a powerful means of influencing a horse.

The spur is used to enhance the leg aid. It should therefore be pushed with varying intensity against the horse's side after the rider's leg has given the aid. While using the spur the leg position should not alter, neither should the rider move his upper body nor interfere with the horse's mouth.

It is most important to keep the hands independent from the spur or whip aid. The whip is usually held with the inside hand so that it lies over the rider's mid-thigh, pointing backwards and downwards. The dressage whip is balanced most effectively with about 10cm (4″) of the handle protruding above the hand.

The whip should be applied with a short turn of the wrist, giving the horse's side a little tap. Like the spur, the whip should be used together with, or after, the leg aid. The whip can only support, never replace, the leg aid.

There are two ways of changing the whip from one side of the horse to the other:

1.   A shortish dressage whip can be changed with one hand holding the whip and both the reins, the free hand pulling the whip slowly and carefully upwards from the other hand. The hand holding the whip then returns to its normal position and takes the rein back from the other hand.

2.   If the dressage whip is too long to be changed in the first method, it is taken 'overhead'. One hand holds the whip and both reins. With a turn of the wrist this hand lifts the long end of the whip. The free hand meets it halfway and takes the whip just below the other hand so that when the hand returns to its own side and retakes its rein the whip is held correctly. The whip must describe a semi-circle in front of the rider's face, and must not touch the horse's head or neck.

If the horse deserves a tap of the whip as punishment, then the reins must be taken into one hand and the whip into the other so as not to pull the horse in the mouth. The tap may only be given close behind the rider's leg.

Changing a short whip

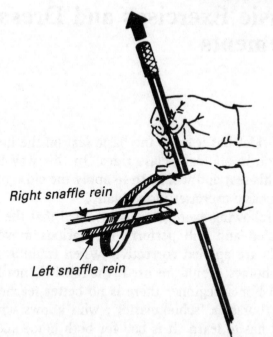

Right snaffle rein

Left snaffle rein

Only an experienced rider should punish a horse. And before he does so he must be absolutely certain as to what caused the horse to be disobedient. In other words, he must assess very quickly whether the horse was actually disobedient, or whether he was overfaced or simply misunderstood the rider's uncertain or incorrect aids. The rider should never lose his temper and punish a horse in anger. An unjust tap with the spur or whip undermines the horse/rider relationship and ruins the horse's trust in his rider. If punishment is justified it has to be immediate, short and determined. Half-hearted efforts confuse the horse and have little effect.

The voice is a very important aid. In the training of young horses one cannot do without it. With older horses the voice should be used sparingly, as otherwise the horse will rely too much on it. Also, when riding in a group it could distract other riders. In dressage competitions the voice aid is prohibited.

4. Basic Exercises and Dressage Movements

After the rider has learned the basic seat on the lunge he should ride in standard class rides. In this way he will establish his seat and will learn to apply the aids correctly by riding basic exercises individually.

In the following exercises it is assumed that the horses are schooled and will perform the various movements if the aids are applied correctly. (When training riders, schooled horses should be used, though it is not always possible.) For a beginner there is no better teacher than a trained horse, a 'schoolmaster', who knows what the rider still has to learn. It is bad for both horse and rider to be beginners. Many spoiled horses and dissatisfied riders are the result of such an unhappy situation, which should be avoided at all costs. Only when a rider has learned on a trained horse what the various movements feel like and how the horse reacts to the correct aids, can he train a green horse.

4(1) Summary of Basic Exercises and Movements

The following are the basic exercises which the rider must learn during his initial training on the flat:

□ Moving off and riding at medium walk.
□ Riding a horse on the bit.
□ Transition from walk to working trot.
□ Working trot, rising; working trot, sitting.
□ Downward transition from trot to walk.

- ☐ Strike-off in working canter from trot.
- ☐ Working canter.
- ☐ Downward transition from canter to trot.
- ☐ Downward transition from walk to halt.
- ☐ Turning on the forehand.
- ☐ Changing rein on straight lines.
- ☐ Working on a circle in all paces.
- ☐ Changing rein out of a circle in walk and trot.

Further Exercises
- ☐ Transitions from one pace to another.
- ☐ Pace variations in trot and canter (extending and reducing the pace).
- ☐ Loops on the long side.
- ☐ Serpentines.
- ☐ Changing rein on a figure of eight.
- ☐ Changing rein through the circle, also simple change of leg.
- ☐ Leg-yielding in the walk.
- ☐ Rein-back.

Final Movements for the Rider's Basic Training
- ☐ Half halt and full halt.
- ☐ Leg yielding in trot.
- ☐ Line to line leg yielding in walk.
- ☐ The volte (small circle of 6m diameter).
- ☐ Half-circle, inclining back to the track.
- ☐ Douple loop on long side.
- ☐ Turn around the haunches.
- ☐ Collected and extended trot and canter.
- ☐ Counter-canter.

The exercises need not be taught in this order. There may be adjustments according to the constitution and ability of horse and rider. But, as in every other training programme, the requirements have to be developed progressively from simple to more difficult exercises.

4(2) **Riding a Horse On the Bit**

First the rider must learn to ride a horse 'on a contact'. This means riding the horse with forward driving leg and seat aids into the hand, until at a halt or in motion the rider feels a definite but gentle contact with the horse's mouth. Only after establishing this contact can the rider maintain control of the horse at all times. However, the contact has to be an elastic one. At times it may have to become a little stronger, but it must never be a 'dead' hold. The moment that the horse accepts the contact, the rider's hand must become 'friendly', or lighten slightly.

Later, when ridden more from behind into the contact, the horse will bring his hind legs forward and closer to his centre of gravity, so that the hind legs carry more weight. As a result of this, the horse on a soft contact will 'give' in the poll, and will be *on the bit*.

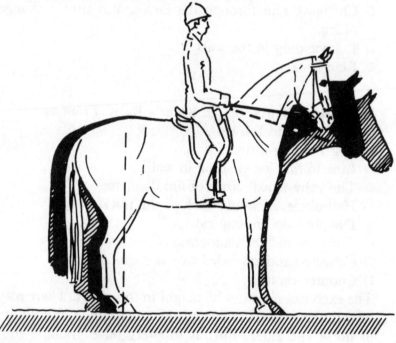

//// Horse standing naturally
■■ Horse on a contact
☐ Horse on the bit

The poll will always be the highest point of the arched neck, and the horse's nose will be carried close to and in front of the vertical. The position which the horse's head and neck should take up will depend on the stage of schooling, the pace, and the degree of collection.

The rider must always remember that the correct and logical way to get a horse on the bit is to ride it from behind forward into the hand. He must not try to force its head and neck into position with rein actions. This would be riding 'backwards' with the hands, and not forward with the legs.

You can tell that a horse is 'on the bit' not only from the position of his head and neck, but from the fact that he is using his back. The activity created by the engaged hind legs must be transmitted through a supple and rounded back and a rounded neck forward into the bit and into the rider's hand.

Should the horse resist and stiffen against the rider's hand the forward driving leg and seat aids should momentarily be increased to encourage the horse to submit to the rider's hand. Afterwards the reins should be yielded slightly. An experienced rider will feel the moment when the horse is going to soften and can yield a little sooner.

The following exercise is a helpful remedy:

Walk the horse on a circle, with stronger inside leg and inside rein. The rein should move slightly inwards, towards the rider's hip – producing a more acute inside flexion and a slight bend. At the same time the supporting outside leg and rein aids must not be forgotten. The moment that the horse submits, the rider's hand must yield again, and the outside rein will again control the horse's bend to the curve of the circle. Since the horse is then *on the bit*, the rider must try to maintain this outline in a slow working trot, and only gradually increase the pace to a normal working trot.

The above is one of many different ways of getting a horse on the bit when he has resisted. Experience will tell a rider which method to apply to the particular horse and circumstances. Remember that *all methods* must have one important factor in common: the horse must be ridden *forward from behind into the hand*, and never pulled backwards with the reins.

4(3) Lateral Flexion and Bend

Lateral Flexion

This happens when the horse turns its head sideways in the axis joint (the joint between head and neck). This is the only part involved: the rest of the spine stays uniformly straight. If flexed to the right, the back edge of the right cheek bone slides under (in rare cases *over*) the parotid glands, and comes closer towards the neck muscles. If the horse is relaxed in the poll and flexes correctly, the crest and mane should 'flip' over towards the inside (in this case the right). The ears should be carried equally high.

To flex a horse laterally the rider, sitting squarely on both seat bones, should ride the horse forward with seat and leg aids into the hand. A little more tension should be created on the inside rein in a sideways/backwards direction, while the outside rein should yield nearly the same amount. To follow up, the inside hand should become light again.

The rider should flex the horse to teach it to submit to the lateral (sideways) influence of the inside rein aid. Not only will the horse submit to the inside rein, but at the same time he will get closer to the outside aids and will learn to accept them (the 'inside' is always the side that the horse is flexed to, independent of what would normally be called the inside or outside in the arena).

If the horse is flexed correctly the rider, sitting straight with equal weight on both seat bones, will see a glimpse of the horse's inside eye and nostril. If the horse is flexed more acutely it will most likely fall out over the outside shoulder, or break the rhythm of the pace.

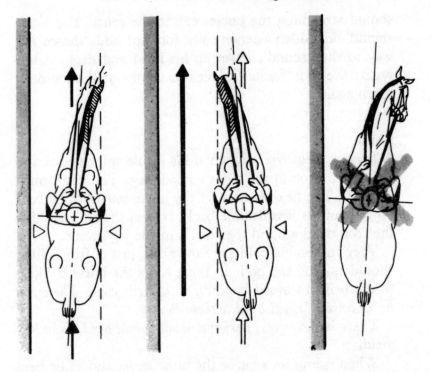

Flexion to right

Flexion to left

Incorrect
Inside hand pulls

When changing the flexion from one side to the other (i.e. when changing rein) the rider must first straighten the horse while riding it actively forward. At the same time he should allow the horse to stretch his nose forward a little so as to give more room to the parotid glands, before flexing the horse in the new direction.

The most common, and also the gravest, fault is a lateral flexion caused by too tight an inside rein. This shortens the horse's neck, making him tense and hard-mouthed, so that his inside hind leg cannot reach sufficiently forward underneath his body.

Another fault is that the new outside rein – i.e. after changing rein – is not yielded sufficiently. The horse will then submit only in the lower jaw, and will not flex in the poll. The head will thus be tilted, one ear carried higher than the other. To correct this fault, the rider should straighten the horse, easing the reins. The horse should be ridden energetically forward and 'shown the way to the ground', lowering his head and neck. Afterwards the aids for lateral flexion in the poll should be given again.

Bend

A horse is bent laterally when his whole spine appears to be curved around the rider's inside leg. The bend must be even. The flexible neck of the horse must not be bent more than his less flexible back. It is in the rib cage that the true bend around the rider's inside leg occurs.

Very vulnerable points are the neck, just in front of the shoulders, and the poll. In these areas the horse is likely to *over*bend to avoid bending in the rib cage. *There can be no correct lateral bend without flexion.*

There is, however, *flexion without lateral bend*, as in leg-yielding.

When riding on a curve the horse must always be bent according to the line it is moving on. His hind legs must

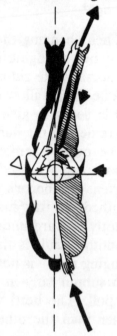

Correct lateral bend to the right

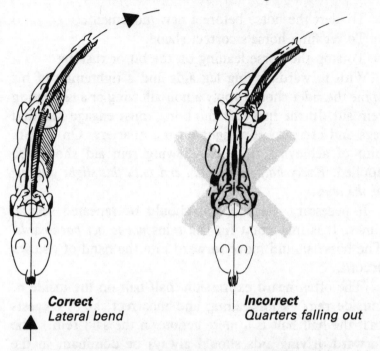

Correct
Lateral bend

Incorrect
Quarters falling out

follow in the tracks of his forelegs, which is achieved by correct timing and by intensity of the diagonal aids:

□ Increased inside leg aid close to the girth.
□ Weight on the inside seat bone.
□ Outside rein controlling the bend in the neck and the flexion in the poll.
□ Inside rein taking and yielding to create flexion.
□ Outside leg supporting behind the girth.
□ The outside aids are often neglected, but they are very important.

4(4) Half Halt and Full Halt

The half halt is used for the following purposes:

□ To prepare for a downwards transition.
□ To slow down the pace.
□ To improve collection or shape of the horse within a pace.

☐ To alert the horse before a new movement.

☐ To regain a horse's correct shape.

☐ To stop the horse leaning on the bit or rushing.

With forward-driving leg aids and a tightening of his spine the rider should apply a non-allowing or a regulating rein aid. In the half halt the horse must engage his hind legs and carry more weight on the quarters. On a mere hint of achieving this, an allowing rein aid should be applied. *Every half halt should end with this slight yielding of the reins.*

If necessary the half halt should be repeated several times. It is important for the reins *not to act backwards.* The horse should move forward into the hand of its own accord.

(The often heard expression 'half halt on the inside or outside rein' is misleading and incorrect, as it suggests that the half halt is a mere action on the said rein.) The forward driving aids should always be dominant in the half halt as it cannot work without them. It can only fulfil its purpose if the hind legs are asked to come closer to the horse's centre of gravity, and if the horse is pushed on a straight line into both, and on circles into the outside rein.

Summing up, it could be said that in a half halt the horse is for a moment increasingly enclosed between leg, weight, and rein aids, when given an allowing rein aid.

The full halt is a series of half halts. It brings the horse to a halt from any pace. When coming to a halt from a fast pace the full halt must be well prepared by half halts.

The full halt is only applied on straight lines. After the horse has come to a halt the rider's hands must ease without losing the contact. While at halt the rider should continue to apply the forward driving leg aids and the tightened spine, but lightly. This prevents the horse from stepping back at halt and ensures that he will stand square and engaged behind.

Correct *'Full halt'*
(transition
to halt)

Incorrect *Rider*
pulling horse
into resistance

Incorrect *Horse*
on forehand

It is important that while halting the horse is still listening to the slight forward driving aids. Only then will he be able to move off at any given pace.

At halt it is very wrong for a rider to move – e.g. by lifting his seat to arrange his jacket, etc. Firstly, this would make it very difficult for the horse to remain immobile. Secondly the horse would no longer 'listen' to the forward driving aids. This would ruin the chances of a smooth move-off after the halt.

When halting, the horse should always be made to stand for a few seconds longer than required.

How strongly the half halt or full halt should be applied depends on the horse's obedience, its stage of training, and the particular circumstances.

4(5) Developing the Paces

The riding horse has three basic paces: walk, trot and canter. There are several variations within each pace, according to the degree of collection and therefore the length of stride.

The regularity of the steps – the rhythm – is of the utmost importance in all three paces.

4(5)i THE WALK

To proceed from halt into walk the rider must first make sure that the horse is standing on the bit. With driving seat and leg aids he should then ask the horse to go forward into walk. His hands should yield the reins slightly without losing the contact.

The walk is a pace of four-time beat. There are three variations in the walk – medium, extended, and collected. In basic training only the medium walk is used. Extended and collected walks are more difficult movements which are only required at a more advanced stage of training.

The Medium Walk

The medium walk is a regular, active and unconstrained pace of moderate extension. The horse's hind feet touch the ground a little in front of the imprints of the forefeet. The horse walks forward calmly with determined steps, while head and neck are unconstrained, lightly on the bit. To maintain a forward walk in clear rhythm the rider should use seat and alternate forward driving leg aids.

4(5)ii THE TROT

To proceed into trot the rider should use the same aids as walking on from a halt, only a little stronger.

The trot is a two-beat pace on alternate diagonals (near fore with off hind and vice-versa) separated by a moment of suspension.

The trot must be free and active, maintaining the rhythm and 'bounce' which originates from a supple back and engaged hindquarters. The horse should be on the bit, champing it mildly, relaxing the lower jaw.

The following are the variations in the trot:

The Working Trot

This is the most suitable trot for a beginner because it allows him to feel and follow the movement. If the rider's seat is inadequate or insecure in working trot, he will interfere least with the free movement of the horse's back.

Working trot is the *hacking* pace, the trot in which the horse works with least effort. It is therefore used when riding out in the countryside, when training young horses, and when warming up for daily work. The regularity of the steps is of the utmost importance. The hind feet meet the imprints of the forefeet.

The Medium Trot

In medium trot the horse's steps cover more ground, but the succession of steps does not become more rapid. There must be obvious impulsion from the hind quarters. The rider allows the horse to lengthen its frame slightly, while keeping the horse on the bit. The horse's hind feet reach a little over the imprints of the front feet – the horse is tracking up.

The Extended Trot

This variation of pace should be ridden only at a more advanced stage of training, when the rider is supple enough to sit to it.

In extending trot – compared with medium trot – there must be a marked accumulation of impulsion, more 'bounce' and maximum ground cover, all emanating from engaged hindquarters. In co-ordination with the increased lengthening of stride there must be a marked lengthening of frame (allowing the nose to stretch a little forwards/downwards while maintaining a contact). The hind feet should reach far beyond the imprints of the forefeet.

The Collected Trot

The collected trot is an advanced movement. It requires excellently timed and correctly applied aids. In this variation of pace the steps are shorter, well marked, and cadenced, the horse moving with a proud head and neck carriage. The haunches and springy hind legs should be engaged and the hind quarters should be lowered and should carry more of the horse's weight. They in turn propel the weight forwards/upwards. This lowering of the quarters enables the horse's shoulders to move with greater ease and fluency in any direction. In relation to the lowering of the haunches is the arching of the neck. It is called 'related' raising and arching of the neck, in contrast to the false 'active' raising and arching of the neck, caused by a forceful rider's hand.

In collected trot the hind feet hardly reach the imprints of the forefeet.

Rising Trot

Correct Seat forward   **Incorrect** Seat backwards

The Rising Trot

This is one of the first lessons that a rider has to learn. It is less tiring for a beginner than the sitting trot. It reduces the impact of the rider's weight on the horse's back, and even a beginner can follow the horse's movement.

In rising trot the rider sits in the saddle for every alternate step. In between, he rises, supported by the stirrups and with his knees relaxed. While coming softly down into the saddle his seat is brought gently forward. While rising he must not actively stand up but swing upwards, keeping his weight as close as possible to the saddle; the weight must sink into his heels. How far the seat leaves the saddle depends on the horse's movement.

The seat returns to the saddle while the inside hind leg is touching down. Simultaneously, the outside foreleg touches down (i.e. the outside diagonal, each diagonal being named after its foreleg).

In an arena the rider should always sit when the inside hind leg and outside foreleg are touching down, as the inside hind leg can then support the weight better, especially in turns. When changing direction the rider therefore has to change diagonals. He can do so by sitting for an extra step. A beginner might find it easier to sit for an uneven number of extra steps.

In rising trot the rider must keep the horse light and definitely on the bit. This means that he must be able to ride the horse on by pushing his hips and seat well forward while coming down into the saddle. At the same moment, he should use his lower legs. Knees and ankle joints should move with suppleness and elasticity.

Only by getting the horse's hind legs to step more forward under his body can the rider improve the horse's pace and suppleness in rising trot.

The horse's outline will deteriorate if the rider's upper body tilts forward; if he allows his seat to slip backwards and his back to become wobbly; if he drops the contact; or if he grips with the knees, holding his ankle joints immobile. A rider gripping with the knee cannot use his lower legs properly.

When hacking, diagonals should be changed at regular intervals so that one of the diagonals is not overworked. This must be done conscientiously, as most horses have a tendency to let the rider sit on the right diagonal. If a rider makes a habit of sitting on one diagonal – for example the right – he could damage the off foreleg, which would constantly be carrying more weight.

The transition from trot to walk should be carried out at sitting trot. The horse is made alert by half halts. To make the transition, the rider should use seat and forward driving leg aids to push the horse into a non-allowing hand. The immediate yielding with the hand – even out of the elbow – together with the forward driving leg aids, will give the horse enough freedom in the neck to walk on energetically.

4(5)iii THE CANTER
The canter is a three-time pace, with each stride separated by a moment of suspension.

The distinction between left and right canter depends on which lateral pair of legs reaches further forward. The following are the variations in canter:

The Working Canter

The variation of the canter is used by the novice rider for the same reasons as the working trot. In the working canter the horse will gain about one horse-length of ground with every stride.

The Medium Canter

The same criteria apply as to medium trot. Compared with working canter there is increased covering of ground without any change of rhythm.

The Extended Canter

In dressage terms this is the canter which gains most ground. Like the extended trot it can only be used at an advanced stage of training.

The Collected Canter

The same criteria apply as to collected trot. In this canter the strides are shorter and have more cadence than in others. The collected canter is the only variation of pace in which the horse is ridden with a slight inward flexion – even on straight lines. In collected canter the horse covers little ground, and it is only with inward flexion that he can maintain rhythm and engaged hind quarters.

The Strike-off in Canter

The horse should be prepared with a half halt, bringing both hind legs closer to his centre of gravity. Collecting the horse like this is necessary to enable him to 'jump' into canter when striking off. At the same time the rider should flex the horse slightly in the direction of the desired canter, left or right. To strike off in right canter the following aids should be applied:

□ The rider's right leg applied close behind the girths causes the horse's right hind leg to reach further forward.

□ The right rein, taking and giving a little, produces flexion at the poll to the right.

□ The left rein controls the degree of flexion and limits the forward stride of the left foreleg.

□ The rider's left leg, lying further behind the girth, controls the quarters and prevents the horse's left hind leg from stepping sideways.

□ The rider's weight should be predominantly on the right seat bone. (The rider must learn to put more weight on to the right stirrup, which will prevent him from collapsing the right hip while trying to put more weight on to the right seat bone.)

□ At the moment of strike-off the rider should ease the right rein to let the horse's stride flow. Forward driving seat and leg aids keep the canter fluent.

□ The rider's upper body must follow the movement. His inside hip should be pushed well forward, but his left, outside, shoulder must not get left behind. His seat should remain softly and constantly in the saddle.

The hands should be held steadily and evenly, following the canter movement, to maintain a steady contact with the horse's mouth. With half halts the rider must keep the canter bouncy and must prevent the horse from 'falling apart', when the canter stride becomes long and flat and the horse is ready to break into trot.

Faulty Seat Positions in Canter
Common faults in a rider's seat positions are:
□ Shoulders drawn up.
□ Stomach pulled in.
□ Gripping up with knee and heel.
□ Unsteady, often too high, hands.
□ Looking down.
□ Collapsing a hip.
□ Outside leg slipping forward.

A noticeable fault is that which occurs after the strike-off, when the rider's outside leg leaves its position and slips forward. This is dangerous, because should the inside leg push a little too hard, the horse could be induced to change the canter. *Remember*: the outside leg must stay in its position further behind the girth to keep in control of the quarters. *During every canter stride the rider must sit as for the strike-off – ready to repeat the canter aid if necessary.*

At first, the canter strike-off is practised from trot. Later it should also be practised from walk. The best place in which to begin a transition is at the first corner of a short side of the school, or if riding on a circle at one end of the school, when returning to the track and to the wall after crossing the arena. At these places the rider will be able to prevent the outside hind leg from deviating outwards in the strike-off.

A relaxed supple strike-off will produce a relaxed and soft canter.

Correcting the strike-off
If the horse strikes off on the wrong leg the rider should make a calm transition to trot. In the trot he can then regain proper control, and with more determined aids can strike off again. When riding in a class ride the rider should leave the track when his horse is in the wrong canter and should make the transition to trot on the inside track.

Lengthening
Lengthening the canter must be carried out fluently and rhythmically. The forward driving aids must not be applied suddenly. With increased lengthening the rider has to go more with the movement. And although the horse is on a definite contact the rider has to keep the horse supple and flexible by applying half halts.

Shortening

The shortening of the canter stride has to be carried out gradually. With forward driving aids the hind legs should be brought further underneath the horse's body, and with half halts they are made to carry more weight. The half halts and subsequent easing of the reins should be applied in rhythm with the canter stride.

With more advanced horses the rider's hands should be rather passive. His legs, however, should further activate the horse's hind legs and create regular, lively strides. Also, in collected canter the rider must feel with his seat the powerful kick-off when the hind legs are leaving the ground.

If the canter pace is shortened solely by regulating rein action, the canter can easily become a four-beat movement – a faulty pace.

To collect the canter stride the rider's inside hand must ease with every stride, allowing each stride to go forward.

If the inside hand does not yield, but maintains an elastic contact in a non-allowing way (together with a tightening of the rider's back, more weight on both seat bones, and forward driving leg aids), the horse will make a transition from canter to trot, walk, or even halt.

This transition must be executed in a clear and fluent manner, finishing with a noticeably yielding hand. When making a transition to walk – as in trot to walk – the rider's hands must visibly move forward, or he should let the reins slip through his hand about 10cm (4"). Then, after the transition the horse can stride out actively.

When advanced riders make a downward transition from canter on a straight line they bring the horse's fore-hand slightly into the school, tending towards shoulder-in, bringing the horse into a shoulder-fore position. (Shoulder-fore is not a school movement, but a training movement; it is a half shoulder-in, and practised before the horse learns shoulder-in.) This is necessary because the horse's forehand is narrower than its quarters. When tending towards shoulder-fore, the horse's inside shoulder should be situated straight in front of its inside hip. In this position the horse's inside hind leg can, during the transition, step further forward towards the centre of gravity and can thus carry more weight.

Simple Change of Leg

A simple change of leg at the canter is at first achieved through trot. Later on, the change is made through walk. A half halt in canter brings the horse directly to walk.

After a number of rhythmic and well-defined walking steps the horse should be cantered on again. The rider should use the walking steps to change his position in order to be able to apply the aids for the other canter and also to change the horse's flexion in the direction of the new canter.

During a progressive training programme the rider will ask for fewer and fewer walking strides. Finally he will be able to make a smooth and straight transition on a straight line from canter to walk – and after only two or three steps will be able to strike off again equally fluently and straight.

Rider Fault

The main rider fault in a simple change is to use only the rein aid or to use it too strongly. This unbalances the canter, forcing the horse on to his forehand, which is unnecessarily strenuous for his forelegs.

Instead of 'hands only' the rider must prepare the downward transition with half halts and forward driving seat and leg aids, to make the horse lighten his forehand and carry as much weight as possible on the hind quarters.

No transition is correctly executed without the logical preparation of half halts.

The Counter-Canter

If a rider is in left canter on the right rein, or vice versa, he is in counter-canter. To achieve counter-canter the rider should canter on the correct lead and then change the rein – e.g. from K to B or with a counter change of hand – and proceed on the new rein without changing the canter. In counter-canter the rider may not ride any sharp turns. The corners should be rounded off slightly.

Counter-canter is ridden only in collected canter. The horse remains flexed towards the side of the leading leg.

It is important for the rider to maintain a positive contact with the supporting outside rein. (In counter-canter on the left rein the 'outside' rein is the *left* one.) This prevents the horse, especially in turns and circles, from falling out over the outside shoulder and adopting an exaggerated flexion in the poll.

Many riders make the mistake of twisting the upper body when in counter-canter. This fault must be eliminated, as it serves no purpose and is even disturbing. Only when sitting correctly can the rider give correct aids. In counter-canter this means an especially quiet upper body position, with hips and shoulders parallel to those of the horse.

4(5)iv THE REIN-BACK

The horse's suppleness and obedience are improved by the rein-back. It also bends and lowers the joints of the hind quarters and thereby helps collection. It may also be used in moderation as a punishment: for example with horses which pull or run out when jumping.

In rein-back the horse steps backwards with alternate diagonal pairs of legs in a straight line without any sideways deviation of a hind leg. The hooves have to leave the ground distinctly.

The footfall of the rein-back is similar to the trot, but the rein-back has no moment of suspension.

During preliminary training an approximate number of steps is required for the rein-back. During more advanced training a specified number of steps is required.

The Aids
The horse must be standing square on a straight line. He must be 'listening' and well 'on the aids'. The rider should then apply forward driving aids with legs and seat. At the moment when the horse wants to step forward he meets the non-allowing rider's hand. (In preliminary training the reins may have to restrict a little more strongly.) This causes the horse to rein back instead of moving forward – 'the forward moving impulse is let out backwards'.

The moment that the horse responds and starts to move backwards the rider's hands must become light, but the contact must not be dropped. Under no circumstances must the horse be pulled backwards. Both of the rider's legs are feeling the horse a little further behind the girth (supporting leg aid) keeping the horse from deviating sideways.

In the rein-back the rider must not sit deep in the saddle, but must transfer some of his weight to the thighs, without leaning forward. With the body in vertical position the rider is able at any time to sit in and use tightening of the back muscles together with forward driving leg aids and easing of the reins to halt the rein-back or to prevent a horse from rushing backwards.

Most common faults in the rein-back are:
☐ A bad halt before asking for the rein-back.
☐ Starting the rein-back with rein aids only.
☐ Rider pulling in his stomach and pulling up his knees.
☐ Leaning forward.
☐ Horse's quarters deviating because rider's legs not sufficiently supportive.
☐ Rider's hand blocking.
☐ Rider sitting too heavily.

4(6) **Turns and Circles**

The rider can ride a turn or circle correctly when he is able to bend the horse's body laterally according to the curvature of the line which he follows. He must be able to cause the hind feet to follow exactly in the tracks of the forefeet.

In a correctly executed turn or circle the horse's inside hind leg carries more weight than the outside one.

Before every turn or circle the rider should prepare the horse with a half halt and transfer his weight a little to the inside seat bone, in the direction of the movement.

The horse should then be flexed in the same direction. The inside rein should guide the horse into the turn, the rider's inside leg, close to the girth, causing the horse's inside hind leg to reach further forward. The outside rein should yield just enough to allow the horse to flex to the inside, while at the same time it restrains the horse from falling out over the outside shoulder. The outside leg should control the quarters.

When the horse's forehand is guided from the straight line into the direction of the turn, the influence of the inside rein is decreased again. The rider should 'straighten' the horse with the outside rein, keeping the horse exactly on the line of the circle. ('Straight' on the circle means making sure that the hind feet follow in the tracks of the forefeet, and that the horse is bent from head to tail according to the curvature of the line.)

The correct distribution of the rider's weight is most important. In transferring his weight to the inside seat bone he should push the inside hip forward with a deep knee. This will also prevent him from collapsing his inside hip and slipping the seat to the outside. At the same time he should make sure not to leave the outside shoulder behind.

Only when sitting correctly with correct distribution of weight can the rider bend his horse as needed.

Riding a Corner

To ride a corner correctly it is necessary to apply a half halt six metres (20 feet) away from the wall ahead. The horse should be flexed to the inside, then the corner should be ridden like a quarter volte (6-metre circle). Aids and bend should be similar to those in riding a circle.

If the horse tries to cut the corner, not bending laterally, the rider must counteract with strong inside aids.

A rider at preliminary stage is advised to practise riding a corner at a walk, and to give the aids one after another rather than simultaneously. Also he should not make the mistake of guiding the horse's head and neck too deep into the corner, thus coming out of it with the wrong bend.

It is also incorrect to ride the horse deeper into the corner by bringing both hands to the outside, with the inside hand crossing the mane. This causes the horse to fall out over the shoulder.

When riding a turn out of doors the rider must ensure that the horse does not try to avoid bending correctly by approaching the turn not on a straight line but on an outward curve.

Before changing rein on the riding school diagonal the rider has to ensure that the horse does not turn too soon. After the corner, inside leg and outside rein keep the horse straight on the track for one horse's length. Only when the horse's outside shoulder reaches the marker should the rider start the turn across the diagonal. If there is no wall the outside aids have to keep the horse on the curvature of the turn and not allow him to fall out.

After each turn the horse should be ridden actively forward.

Riding a Circle

When riding on a circle the horse's hind quarters must be guided and controlled by the rider's legs; his forehand

Riding a Corner

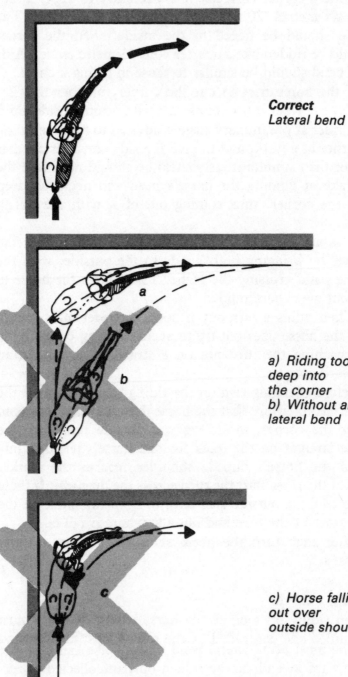

Correct
Lateral bend

*a) Riding too
deep into
the corner
b) Without any
lateral bend*

*c) Horse falling
out over
outside shoulder*

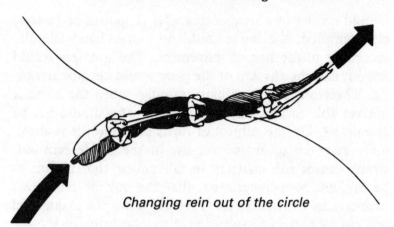

Changing rein out of the circle

by the reins. The circumference of the circle is determined by the circle markers.

The rider's inside leg, close behind the girth, activates the inside hind leg, helping to maintain the lateral bend and preventing the horse from falling into the circle. The rider's outside leg should be positioned further behind the girth, controlling the quarters. The rider's outside leg, together with the inside rein, should maintain the lateral bend and cause the outside hind leg to step further forward.

When changing rein on a figure of eight the horse should be straightened for a moment before flexing and bending him in the new direction. The same applies for changing 'through' the circle. The rider must be careful not to ride too wide a first half-circle so that the second half-circle can be of equal diameter.

When changing either out of or through the circle the rider must shorten the new inside rein, transferring his weight to the new inside seat bone, and changing the leg aids accordingly.

The Volte
The volte is a small circle 6m (20ft) in diameter. It calls for the most acute lateral bend that a horse can perform on one track, and can be ridden only in collected paces.

Should a volte of a smaller diameter (5 metres or 16 feet) be attempted, the horse could no longer bend laterally according to the line of movement. The quarters would fall out and the rhythm of the pace would become irregular. Therefore in preliminary training, when the horse is not yet able to move in collection, a volte should not be attempted. On the subject of turns or circles, it is absolutely essential to avoid over-use of the inside rein aid, which causes the quarters to fall out or the rhythm to be broken. Remember, too, that the outside rein must maintain an elastic contact. Pressing down the inside heel will ensure correct distribution of weight, bringing it more on to the inside seat bone.

Otherwise the aids for riding a volte are the same as for riding a circle.

The most common rider fault when riding a volte is to change its shape into an oval. The volte must be absolutely round and must end where it began. A novice rider can make sure of this by placing the volte intentionally a little in front of where it touches the track.

To improve this movement it is helpful to ride a few voltes, one after another, in the same place.

Half-Circles

When riding a half-circle and inclining back to the track, the aids for the first part of the movement are the same as for the volte. A half-volte is ridden in a 5m (16ft) diameter. It is usually ridden in the second corner of a long side. At the widest part of the half-volte the rider inclines towards a straight line back to the track, touching the same 10.50m (35ft) after the corner.

Loops

Depending on their number and size, loops are used either as exercises for making the horse supple or as preparation for collection. The number of loops to be ridden depends

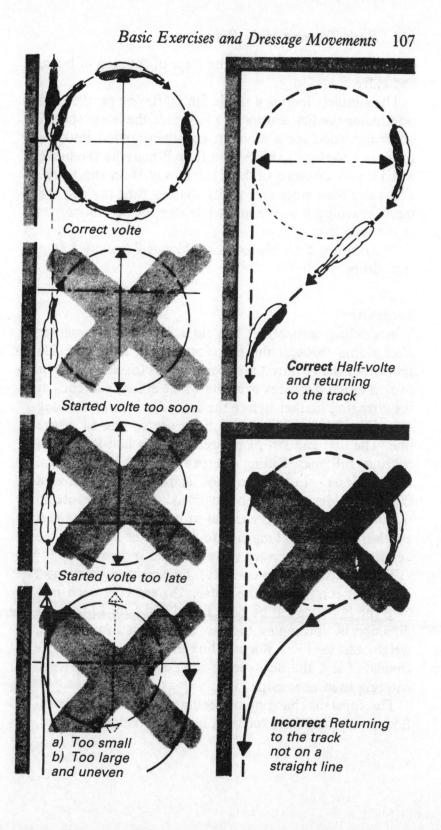

Correct volte

Started volte too soon

Started volte too late

a) Too small
b) Too large
and uneven

Correct Half-volte
and returning
to the track

Incorrect Returning
to the track
not on a
straight line

on the size of the arena and the stage of training of horse and rider.

The simplest loop is a single 5m (16ft) one on the long side. After the first corner of a long side the horse should be straightened for a moment and then guided into the arena in a shallow loop. At the E or B markers the horse will be at a distance of 5m (16ft) away from the track. The rider then rides an equally shallow turn back to the track, reaching it at the marker before the second corner of the long side.

When riding a double loop each loop will be only 2.50m (8ft) deep.

Serpentines
When riding serpentines the rider turns at the marker after riding through the first corner of a long side. He spaces out the required number of loops (usually three or five) at equal distances over the whole arena, and ends at the changing marker before the second corner of the long side. The loops are counted from centre line to centre line. The first and last loops are then only half-loops, but count as full ones. Riding a serpentine as in international competitions – i.e. starting and ending at the centre of the short side – should be avoided. This is because in training horses it is very useful to be able to use the first and last corner of a long side to prepare the horse for the bending that is necessary when riding a serpentine.

To ride a serpentine correctly the weight aids are most important for turning the horse. On entering each new loop the horse has to be both flexed and bent in the new direction by shortening the new inside rein and changing weight and leg aids. When riding in canter with a simple change of leg, the new canter should be asked for when entering each new loop.

The constant changing of flexion and bend in a serpentine is very beneficial for both horse and rider.

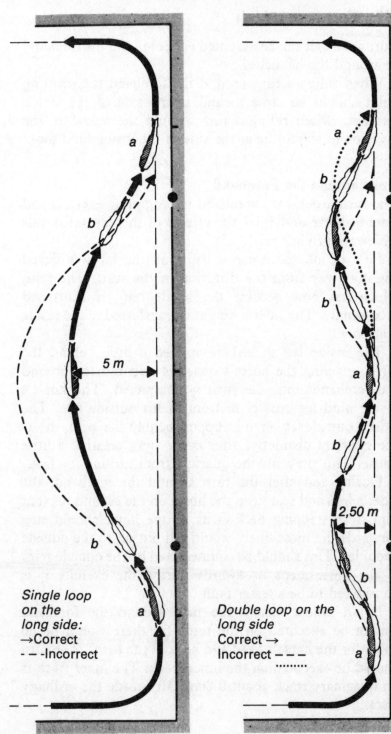

Single loop
on the
long side:
→Correct
- - -Incorrect

5 m

Double loop on the
long side
Correct →
Incorrect - - - -
....

2,50 m

a/b) Changing the bend   *a/b) Changing the bend*

4(7) **Turns at a Halt**

Turns at a halt can be executed either around the forehand or around the haunches.

When riding a turn around the forehand the pivoting point should be close to and at the side of the inside forefoot. When riding a turn around the haunches the pivot point should be at the side of the inside hind foot.

Turn around the Forehand

The turn around the forehand is a suppling exercise and teaches horse and rider the effects of the one-sided aids (sideways driving aids).

First of all, the horse – being on the bit – is flexed slightly away from the direction of the turn. The rein, which has now become the inside rein, is shortened accordingly. The rider's weight is transferred to the inside seat bone.

The inside leg should be applied a little behind the girth, pushing the horse's quarters step by step around the forehand until the turn is completed. The horse's inside hind leg crosses in front of his outside one. The rider's outside leg, giving support behind the girth, meets the quarters distinctly, after every step, creating a little pause. This prevents the quarters from turning too fast.

During and after the turn around the forehand, the rider's legs and seat keep the horse on the bit and prevent him from stepping backwards. If the horse should step forwards, he most likely would fall out on to the outside shoulder. This should be counteracted by the outside rein. If the horse steps backwards during the exercise it is considered to be a lesser fault.

In an indoor school the turn around the forehand cannot be executed on the track (as there would be no room for the horse's head and neck in the turn). The turn should be executed on the inner track. The inner track is an imaginary track about 0.80m (3ft) inside the ordinary track.

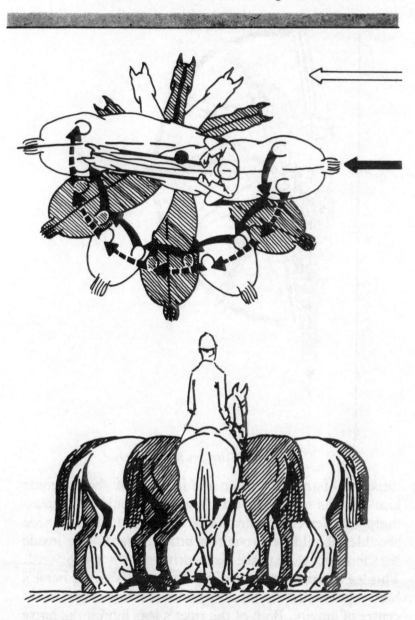

Turn on the forehand

Turns around the Haunches

The turn around the haunches creates collection. First of all, the horse – on the bit – should be flexed well in the

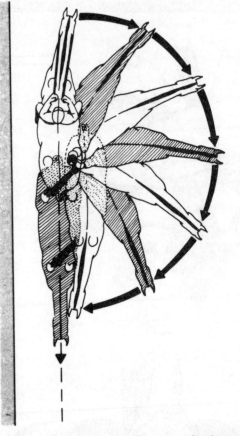

Turn on the haunches

direction of the turn, then the inside rein should guide
him into the turn. The rider's weight should be increasingly transferred to the inside seat bone. The outside
shoulder should be brought a little forward. The inside
leg should act close to the girth, driving the horse forward.
This leg and the supporting outside leg activate the horse's
hind legs to step rhythmically forward and closer to his
centre of gravity. Both of the rider's legs inhibit the horse
from stepping backwards; the outside supporting leg prevents the outside hind foot from deviating sideways.

The outside rein should control the amount of flexion,
but must yield enough so that the horse can move uninter-
rupted in the direction of the turn.

In this movement it is essential for the hind legs to maintain an even and regular 4-beat rhythm.

It is a minor fault if the horse steps a little forward. For a novice rider it is even advisable to start the turn by asking the horse to take one or two small steps forward, and only then to begin the turn around the haunches.

Since the pivoting point of this movement is at the side of the inside hind leg, the horse, in executing the turn, leaves the track and ends the movement his own width away from the track. Therefore he has to be guided forwards/sideways back on to the track while completing the last step of the turn. In this way it is possible to finish the movement correctly, with the horse standing squarely on the track, after the turn around the haunches.

Main rider faults in the turn around the haunches are:
□ Too much outside leg.
□ Wrong displacement of the weight (on to the outside seat bone).
□ Collapsing the inside hip.
□ Too much rein action.
These faults usually happen together and cause the horse to step backwards and flex incorrectly, against the direction of the turn.

4(8) Turns at a Pace

The turn around the haunches, executed at any pace, is called a HALF-PIROUETTE.

At elementary level a pirouette is performed at a walk or collected trot. (When performed at a collected trot the actual turn is also executed at walk.) The horse may not come to a halt before or after the turn. The aids are the same as in the turn around the haunches.

The half-pirouette has the advantage that the horse is already moving forward. It is easier, therefore, to prevent the horse from standing on the inside hind leg or even stepping backwards during the turn.

114 Basic Training of the Rider

4(9) Leg-yielding

Leg-yielding is the most basic of all lateral movements. It is a suppling exercise, making the horse loose and unconstrained, and teaching him to obey the sideways driving aids. It is an excellent means of teaching the novice rider to co-ordinate his aids.

When leg-yielding, the horse is straight from head to tail, with a slight flexion away from the direction in which he is moving. He moves forward/sideways on two tracks. The inside legs pass and cross in front of the outside legs.

Since the horse is flexed towards the sideways driving leg, this side is called his 'inside', even if it is facing the outside of the arena.

Leg-yielding can be performed at a walk or – for a short distance – at a trot, on the long sides of the school, on the diagonal, and on the circle.

When leg-yielding along the long side of the school, the novice rider or horse should start by yielding from the leg facing the wall. When facing the wall at an angle it is easier for horse and rider to get the effect of the sideways driving aids.

Later on it will be found more beneficial to leg-yield from the inside leg along the wall, with the horse facing the inside of the school.

When leg-yielding along the edge of the school the horse should be at a maximum angle of 45° to the wall.

The Aids

The rider should sit more on the inside seat bone, with his inside leg close behind the girth, pushing the quarters sideways. This leg aid should be applied at the moment when the inside hind leg is lifted off the ground to start a forward/sideways step. If necessary the aid is repeated with every step or stride. The forehand is guided along its track by the outside rein. By supporting action of the outside leg the rider counteracts any rushing away from

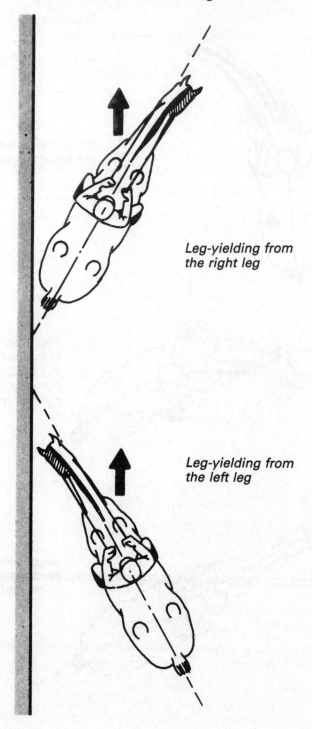

Leg-yielding from
the right leg

Leg-yielding from
the left leg

Incorrect leg-yielding

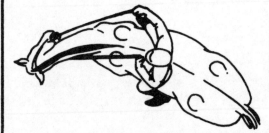

Horse falling out over
the left shoulder

Too much bend
in the neck.
Horse falling
out over the
right shoulder.

Angle too large.
No flexion
in the poll.

the inside leg, and with the supporting outside rein he eliminates any falling out on to the outside shoulder.

When planning to leg-yield along the wall of the school, with the horse's head towards the wall, the rider should start the move in the first corner of a long side. As soon as the horse's head reaches the wall of the long side, the rider should apply a half halt. The fact that the horse is slightly facing the wall will help the half halt to have effect (which is another essential reason why this kind of leg-yielding should be taught first to novice riders and/or horses). The horse should then be straightened and flexed towards the wall. From this position the rider should start the leg-yield.

To finish the leg-yield the horse should be flexed the other way and the forehand should be guided in a shallow turn to align with the hind quarters. The rider should then proceed straight ahead, and only at this point should he return to the track.

When leg-yielding along the wall from the leg which is facing the inside of the school, the rider should lead the forehand a step into the school as though he wanted to change the rein on the diagonal. The quarters should stay on the track. The rider should then apply a half-halt and start leg-yielding. To end the leg-yielding he should bring the forehand back to the track in line with the quarters.

Line-to-Line Leg-Yielding

To test and improve the horse's obedience to the forward/-sideways driving leg aid and the guiding outside rein, leg-yielding from line to line is a good exercise.

In Germany this exercise is carried out from the long side, about 5m (16ft) inwards and then back to the track.

It should be ridden in walk or working trot. The horse moves on two tracks, which are one step apart, with a slight flexion away from the direction of movement nearly parallel to the long side of the arena. The forehand should be slightly in advance of the quarters.

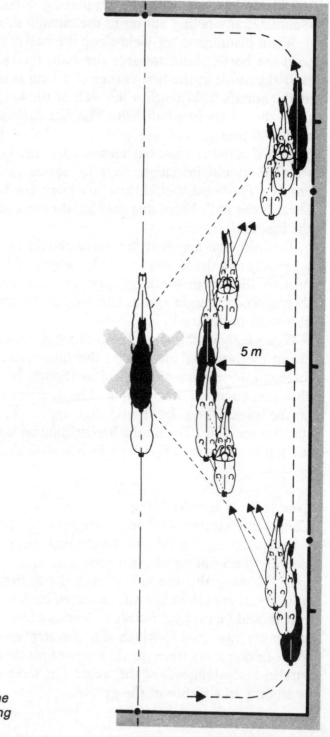

5 m

*Line-to-line
leg-yielding*

After passing the first corner of a long side the rider should straighten the horse for a moment. At the marker, he should flex the horse away from the direction of movement. Then he moves the horse with the – now – inside leg forward/sideways into the arena. The outside leg together with the weight aids keep the horse going well forward and prevent the quarters from preceding the forehand.

The leg-yielding on the first diagonal into the arena is finished when the horse's head is nearly in line with the middle of the long side. He is by then about 5m (16ft) away from the wall. Here the horse is ridden straight ahead for one horse's length. The flexion should then be changed to the opposite side and the rider's leg should yield the horse back towards the track, which he should meet at the marker before the corner of the long side.

5. Jump Training

In Germany a correct systematic training in basic dressage is considered to be the prerequisite for successful jumping. The rider also has to learn to sit perfectly in an independent balanced forward seat from which he is able to control the horse with dressage aids.

The logic of training to jump is the same for horse and rider in general schooling: start with simple demands and progress gradually.

For the education of a rider, training on uneven terrain and over jumps is as important as flat riding. They are not only a valuable addition to flat riding but the best means of familiarizing the rider with his horse, relaxing them both and developing mutual confidence. The main phases in the jump training of the rider are:

☐ Familiarizing the rider with the feel of the horse's movement on uneven terrain.
☐ Working over cavaletti, riding with shorter stirrups (light seat).
☐ Learning and perfecting the forward seat position. Canter in forward seat position on flat and uneven going.
☐ Jumping single fences.
☐ Riding through a jumping lane (gymnastic jumping).
☐ Riding a course of show jumps out of doors and jumping cross-country fences.

5(1) Work over Cavaletti

Cavaletti are poles 2.50m (8ft) to 3.50m (11ft) in length, supported at each end by timber crosses. (See diagram on page 122.) They can be used at three different heights:

(a) Upside down, with the pole on the ground.

(b) On their side, height 25cm (10in.).

(c) Standing up, height 40cm (16in.).

Work over cavaletti is mostly carried out at walk or in trot, and, later on, occasionally in canter.

Initially riders are asked to walk their horses over single poles on the ground. Later the horses are worked at walk and in trot, over poles on the ground or over cavaletti on their side (position B). When rider and horse are able to negotiate these, still maintaining balance and rhythm, a row of cavaletti is laid out: at first only two or three, later on up to six, all 1.3m (4ft 3in.) apart. They are first placed on the track, to give horse and rider the security of the wall on one side and to facilitate the approach. Later on they may be used in the centre of the school or on the diagonal, but with wings on both sides, at least for the first cavaletti. Since the distance is set at 1.3m (4ft 3in.) the row may only be used in trot.

The cavaletti are first used upside down (position A). They may gradually be raised one by one to position B.

During work over cavaletti the rider is given the opportunity of feeling the sensation of the horse's swinging back as he trots over the poles. The rider will feel that he must be very balanced and supple in his seat so as not to interfere with the horse's exaggerated trot over the cavaletti. To make it easier for the horse to use his back he has to be allowed to lower his head and neck. To achieve this, therefore, the rider must learn to move his hands forwards/downwards along the horse's shoulders.

A nervous or temperamental young horse may at first try to jump the single cavaletti. The rider should anticipate this and be careful not to be unbalanced and thereby disturb the horse in the mouth or back. Only when a horse is relaxed can the row of cavaletti be attempted.

The seat position adopted when riding over cavaletti depends on the purpose of the exercise and the ability of the rider. It should be either a rising trot or a sitting trot; the latter only in light seat position, easing the weight in

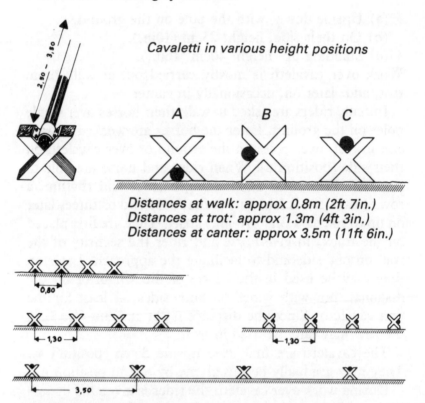

Cavaletti in various height positions

Distances at walk: approx 0.8m (2ft 7in.)
Distances at trot: approx 1.3m (4ft 3in.)
Distances at canter: approx 3.5m (11ft 6in.)

the saddle. Cavaletti work in canter should be carried out in forward seat only. For this the cavaletti are positioned 3.50m (11ft 6in.) apart and may be at their full height (position c).

5(2) Improving the Forward Seat

Cantering in forward seat position must be practised frequently in order to master the balance and control which will be required in future jump training.

The rider should start canter work on a circle, go on to straight lines – shortening and lengthening the stride – and should finally practise turns. All turns must be ridden with strong supporting outside leg and rein aids – *never* by pulling the horse around with the inside rein and dropping the outside one.

The jumping seat

Only when correctly ridden will the horse be able to turn on his hind legs and move energetically forward after the turn is completed. And only in this way will the rider acquire *safe, unconstrained control* of the horse, which is obviously necessary when jumping a course.

At a later stage, single and double fences should be introduced into the canter work. The horse will by then take them in his stride without pulling or becoming excited. When approaching a fence the horse must remain calm and relaxed and not lose the canter rhythm.

In perfecting the forward seat the rider must learn to follow the horse's movement at all times in a soft and supple seat position with a light and independent hand position.

5(3) Jumping Single Fences

Having practised the forward seat in canter, the novice rider should be able to begin jumping.

The instructor must make it easy for him to find his balance and to develop 'feel' for jumping.

If suitable horses and conditions are available it is best to start the rider off by jumping small fences from a quiet canter. This is the easiest pace to enable the rider to stay with the horse's movement over a jump. But later on he also will have to practise jumping from trot.

There should be a great deal of variety in jump training. Continuously jumping the same fence at the same location is of little benefit, and will bore both horse and rider.

Every obstacle – either in training or in competition – must be fair and inviting. All fences should have wings. Narrow fences without wings are simply obedience tests and are not suitable for novice jump training. They are unnatural obstacles and will tempt all but the most trusting and experienced horses to run out.

At this stage of training the fence approach should not pose any problem. Therefore the fence must be constructed so that the horse is not tempted to run out or refuse. The rider can thus concentrate on himself and on the job in hand – jumping.

In more advanced training the rider has to learn to cope with difficult approach lines to fences.

Beginners should ride with stirrups and should feel safe when jumping. The stirrups should be adjusted at least four or five holes shorter than for dressage.

It is important for the rider to learn from the beginning to be supple and to absorb the movement of the horse. The rider's upper body should be bent at the hip bones a little forward over the horse's neck. The hands should remain deep against the horse's withers, yielding as required, to allow the horse to bascule over the fence.

Under no circumstances should the rider's lower leg change position. This is vital, as on landing, the rider must absorb the shock with springy knees and heels. Immediately after landing he must also be able to slightly straighten his body and continue to ride in the correct forward seat position.

If in the beginning a rider has trouble in staying with the horse's movement he should catch hold of the mane or a neckstrap. Only when a safe, secure and confident seat is established, can a rider occasionally be asked to jump small fences without stirrups.

Jumping from trot
Especially valuable in the training of horse and rider is the jumping exercise from trot. The fences should not be too difficult, and no higher than 80cm (2ft 6in.).

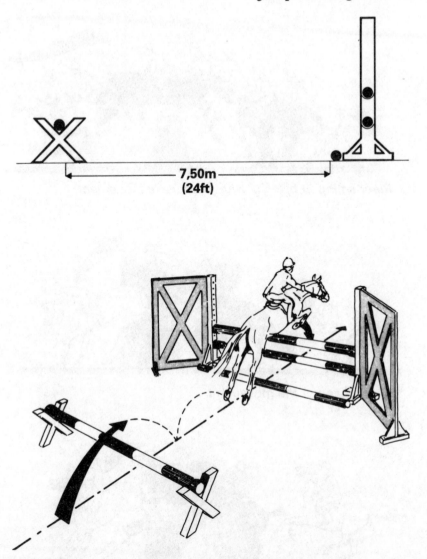

Jumping from trot relaxes the horse, improving his agility and athletic ability, as he has to jump off his hocks. It is also an excellent exercise for improving the rider, as he must follow the horse's movement. The rider has to be quick to move his upper body forward and to close his knees – while keeping them elastic – acquiring a steady lower leg position. When jumping from trot he also has a good opportunity of learning to keep his hands deep,

Rider sitting in balance with the horse's movement

Rider ahead of the movement

Rider left behind

letting them follow the horse's movement forwards/downwards during the jump.

While maintaining a contact, the horse must be given enough rein to be able to stretch his head and neck forwards/downwards over the jump.

The instructor should take great care to see that the rider approaches each fence, either from trot or canter, on a straight line, in the centre, and at an angle of 90°.

When the horse is keen in the approach the rider has to learn to control the pace, but still has to yield the reins a little while maintaining a contact and riding the horse forward. These forward driving aids become even more important if the horse is hesitant in his approach to the fence. It is wrong to approach even the simplest fences carelessly, without any forward driving aids, as this would tempt the horse to refuse or to run out. The forward driving aids have to be applied in rhythm with the canter movement.

The experienced rider can see if he is on a good stride a short distance away from the fence. He can readjust the stride if necessary, to reach the right take-off point. If a less experienced rider notices that his stride is wrong he must ride energetically forward, lengthening the last few strides, and if necessary bringing the take-off point a little closer to the jump. Correcting and adjusting the strides by sending the horse forward makes for fluent jumping, and is more profitable than holding the horse back with the reins to accommodate an additional stride. Adjusting the distance to the fence should always be *forward*.

The get-away after the jump must also be practised with the pupil. He has to learn to proceed on a straight line after the jump and to regain control of the horse and of his own balance as quickly as possible.

If a horse is very lazy, the rider might carry a short whip. It should be used behind the forward driving leg to emphasize the aid – but as the whip is short the rider must first take the reins in one hand, and then use the whip with the other. The short whip may not be used with the rein in the whip hand, as it would interfere with, and jerk, the horse in the mouth. If a novice rider has problems in getting his horse forward into a fence it might be advisable to ask an experienced rider to give him a lead over the fence.

5(4) Gymnastic Jumping

When a rider has acquired an elastic, balanced seat over cavaletti and single fences, he can progress to gymnastic jumping.

A JUMPING LANE is an excellent means of schooling horse and rider. This can consist of a row of six to eight fences, the first few as bounces, then one, two, or three strides between the following fences. At the beginning of the lane the fences must be small (40–60cm or 1ft 6in.–2ft) progressively increasing towards the end of the row.

The distances between the elements depend on three main factors:

☐ The sizes and temperaments of the horses.
☐ The speed of approach (trot or slow canter).
☐ The size of the fences.

The average distances for horses approaching the row *out of canter* are:

☐ 3.50m (11ft) for a bounce.
☐ 7.50m (25ft) for one non-jumping stride.
☐ 10.50m (34ft) for two non-jumping strides.
☐ 14.00m (46ft) for three non-jumping strides. This is the maximum number of strides. When jumping *out of*

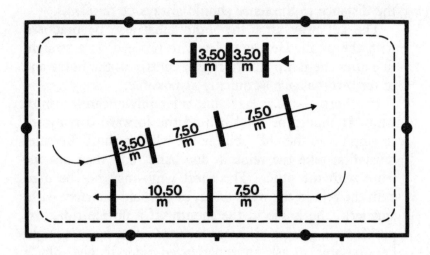

trot, the distances between the first two elements should be shortened accordingly.

The use of spread fences alternating with uprights, with varying distances between elements, teaches riders to be supple and agile in following the horse's movement. Riders also develop a feeling for the correct take-off point.

The fact that the fences in the line come up so swiftly one after another will quicken the rider's reactions. He will only be able to negotiate the sequence satisfactorily if he creates and maintains the proper speed, and will thus learn to feel the correct rhythm and speed for jumping.

Of course, a rider will only benefit if the horse jumps the line of fences correctly. The trainer will therefore have to place wings at each fence, making sure that the horse cannot run out, even if his rider makes a mistake. For a horse which is over-keen in the approach, trotting poles should be used to dictate the proper speed and straight approach.

5(5) Riding a Show Jumping Course

Practising over a full show jumping course must not be left until the actual competition. Problems should be anticipated, prepared for, and remedied well in advance. Regrettably this is often neglected, due to lack of material or time. Show jumping 'training' is so often a schooling session over a few fences, put up casually somewhere without a logical plan. Such a casual programme will not achieve success. It is therefore important to practise over a full course of show jumps.

The first requirement is to learn to ride the correct course-line between fences, approaching each fence on a straight line while maintaining an even canter rhythm between the fences.

To instill in a rider a feeling for prescribed time allowances it is a good idea to measure a course and to time the round correctly.

The rider must also learn to land over a jump in the correct canter for the next turn. If he lands in the wrong canter he must quickly make a simple change through trot.

6. Cross-Country Riding

Riding and jumping across country are an important part of training. It is refreshing and relaxing for both horse and rider. A rider is in full control of his horse only if he is proficient in all paces over any country.

6(1) Cross-Country Training

Before taking pupils out to school across country the instructor must check the terrain and build or rebuild suitable fences.

Cross-country training should begin fairly early, as soon as safety permits. At first, the instructor will bring his class out to a large field or arena, where the pupils can spread out and ride in open order in all three paces. Also included should be walking periods, halting, standing relaxed, mounting and dismounting.

When riding in open spaces local by-laws and other users must be respected.

Training sessions can include the following:

□ Cantering in forward seat singly across flat, later hilly, country.
□ Riding in a group across varying country and through woods.
□ Climbing up and down hills, mounds, and quarries.
□ Walking through and jumping ditches.
□ Walking through and crossing streams.
□ Jumping various cross-country fences.
□ Completing roads and tracks in a set time.

Gradual intensification of a progressive cross-country training programme will soon improve both the horse's

Obstacles suitable for cross-country training

and the rider's confidence. Weather and going permitting, this training should continue all the year round.

Jump training across country is important, because the fences can be built more naturally, blending in with the countryside. The fences should be solid, so that they will be respected by the horse and therefore jumped more cleanly. The fences preferably should have a natural wing on each side – built into an existing hedge, sunken road, woodland clearing, etc. Combinations of a simple fence (poles) with slopes, ditches and banks are interesting and make horse and rider look and think.

There is no set rule as to how to approach cross-country fences. Galloping at a fence from a distance is nearly always wrong. Controlling the pace and riding the last few strides energetically forward is nearly always successful. Even the smallest fence must never be approached carelessly, as it would make the horse uncertain and give him a chance to refuse, or to attempt to jump it so care-

Riding uphill

lessly that he makes a serious mistake.

Climbing or descending a hill must always be done vertically, as diagonally the horse might slip.

When going up or down hill the rider must ease the weight on the horse's back by leaning his upper body forward.

Jumping or crossing water often poses psychological problems for horse and rider. First of all, both must gain confidence at this type of fence. A start should be made with shallow water which has firm footing. An experienced lead horse and rider will teach others to go into water first at walk, then also in trot and canter. Only when horse and rider carry this out confidently can they start to jump out of water and later into it.

Riding downhill

Riding up and down a slope

When approaching an obstacle which involves jumping into water, the rider must control and reassure his horse with firm aids, shortening the stride. This way the horse when entering the water above his knees will not buckle on landing. Neither will he plunge through in panic if the speed of approach does not allow him to see where he is going. Either fault would undermine his confidence for further water-jumps.

The training of a cross-country rider is more successful with an experienced horse. Even on the best horse, however, an inexperienced rider must never practise cross-country unsupervized, but always under the watchful eye of his trainer or some other experienced person.

Jumping on to a bank

6(2) Trekking and Long-Distance Riding

Rides involving a few days' journey call for careful planning. Weekend rides should be within a 50km (31 mile) radius of the rider's home yard. Long-distance rides take longer and cover a greater distance.

Both horse and rider have to prepare carefully for such outings. To achieve a good performance systematic training is needed. The rider must get fit by riding frequently for long periods, and by long trotting sessions. A tired rider is a heavy burden for any horse.

Even a temporary weight relief increases the horse's performance considerably, so the rider must be able to run on foot for long distances. This will be a welcome break for both him and his horse. Since climbing is much more strenuous than going on level ground, it is a particular relief for the horse if the rider dismounts and leads him up a steep hill. The same goes for long descents.

The horse's tack also requires special attention, since on long-distance rides an extra pack has to be carried. Putting this together and securing it to the saddle should be practised in advance.

In preparation for a long-distance ride the horse's physical condition – breathing, temperature and pulse – should regularly be monitored.

The horse should be shod at least eight days before an

outing. Horses with bad feet are obviously not suitable for long-distance riding.

Careful planning for the different stages of the outing is necessary for success. A short distance ridden thoughtlessly wastes more energy than a longer distance making clever use of pace, speed and rest periods.

Groups of riders travel best in two's, respecting the rules of the road. In darkness, the group must carry white lights in front and red ones at the rear.

Food for horse and rider depends on energy output. Frequent small meals are more suitable than a few large ones. Overnight stays must be organized ahead.

The best preparation for long-distance riding is good tuition.

6(3) Hunting

In Germany there are no foxhunting or stag hunting as in other European countries such as England, Ireland and – within limits – France. Various drag hunts are held, but only a relatively small number of riders are able to take part. Therefore German riding schools and clubs organize simulated hunts – ride-outs with one rider out front as 'the fox', then the normal field order. In this way a lot of people have the opportunity to gallop together and learn the disciplines involved.

The following are a few essential points to note:

☐ If the rider loses control of his horse he must leave the hunting field.

☐ If a horse refuses, the rider must quickly make room for other riders to jump the fence.

☐ In the event of a fall, the rider should try to 'roll' but hold on to the reins. A loose horse endangers other riders.

Cherished traditions which have evolved and survived over centuries, especially in hunting nations, should wherever possible, be respected and kept alive.

SECTION TWO
Basic Training of the Horse

1. Notes for the Trainer

In contrast to the first part of the book, this section assumes that the horse's rider and trainer are able to fulfil all the necessary requirements. A young horse *must* be ridden by an experienced rider, otherwise the result is a badly schooled, tense, and disobedient horse. This in turn leads to the frustration, disappointment and discouragement of all concerned.

1(1) Character and Temperament of the Horse and Principles of Training

To avoid overfacing the horse physically or psychologically – with destructive consequences – a trainer must not only have the necessary technical knowledge, but also knowledge of basic animal psychology as well as empathy with his horse. A horse's temperament can be quickly and permanently spoiled by unskilled handling. Retraining will take months, often years. The most obvious consequences of mismanagement are premature wear and tear, especially to the legs.

A horse should have completed its third year (i.e. be approaching four) before being asked to work. It then takes at least a year to school a horse to preliminary level.

The trainer should consider the following points as a psychological guideline:

☐ The horse is a gregarious animal; a highly developed 'running' animal. It feels most secure among members of its own species.

☐ The trainer, recognizing the herd instinct of the horse, assumes the role of leader in the hierarchy.

☐ This position cannot be achieved by force, but only

with firm understanding. When a horse makes a mistake it is most likely caused by misunderstanding the command of the herd leader, rather than by an insubordinate disobedience.

☐ A horse will not accept man's commands without first cultivating trust in him. Trust is the foundation of understanding.

☐ Man's communication with the horse is transmitted through the aids and the auxiliary aids – voice, touch, weight and rewards.

☐ True understanding is achieved by patiently getting the horse used to the aids. The horse – by nature an animal of flight – must be familiarized gradually with strange and unknown objects. If during training uncertainty or even fear develops, you must start again, remembering that the horse has an excellent memory. It can take a long time before a horse forgets the trauma of a bad experience.

☐ A pre-condition for the horse's capacity to learn is his degree of physical maturity. Overtaxing his capacity at any stage brings about an automatic relapse in the training programme.

☐ The horse will achieve his full potential only if he is trained in a happy environment, in which the trainer and his facilities blend to extract the best efforts from the horse.

☐ Contact with man must in all situations represent to the horse security, safety and shelter. Furthermore, the trainer must understand how responsive each of the various horse senses are.

A horse's sense of smell is its best developed sense, but in training it is not of major significance. It can, however, have a negative influence if, because of an unpleasant smell (pigs, goats), or if a certain smell (smoke, chemicals) recalls an unpleasant memory, a horse becomes disobedient.

A horse's hearing is also well developed. That is why

unnecessary noise in the stable and during training should be avoided. The exceptional mobility of the horse's ears allows him to direct them towards any noise source without moving his head.

A horse's eyesight is not particularly well developed. Unlike man, who has an eye-ball with an adjustable optic lens which focuses objects on his retina, the horse has a fixed lens in front of a ramped retina, so he must adjust his entire head position to focus on objects (i.e. lift his head to focus on distant objects, lower his head to focus on close objects, such as a strange fence). A horse can often see a distant moving object more quickly than his rider, who therefore may not realize why the horse is getting excited or starting to shy.

A horse's sensitivity to touch, with lip whiskers as well as his overall skin sensitivity, is very well developed. It is important to understand this in order to apply the correct touch aids, not only in training but in later work.

To a keen trainer the movements of the horse's eyes, ears and tail; his nostrils blowing; and sweat patches; are all tell-tale signs of the animal's psychological condition. A horse's eye is the reflection of his mental condition and attitudes. It can show fear, good nature, attentiveness, or mistrust.

The horse's ear movements can also say a lot about his mental condition. Ears flat back always display acute mistrust and are a defence posture. Lively and pricked ears display attentiveness and are an indication that the horse is willing to co-operate.

A horse snorting contentedly, with a well-carried tail moving freely from side to side denotes relaxed, unconstrained muscles and the horse's willingness to work. A high or tense tail carriage indicates that the horse is excited or frightened.

A horse sweats not merely because of work exertion

but sometimes through excitement or fear. This is usually combined with raised pulse and breathing rates.

It is most important for the trainer to work quietly and calmly at all times. Highly-strung people are often impatient and lack the necessary self-control and objectivity to achieve satisfactory results.

Constant repetition of all activities necessary for safe conduct with a horse – such as tying up, picking out feet, leading, or standing up will establish his positive reflexes.

Praise, scolding, or sometimes even punishment must be used as educational aids only in direct relation to the expected or produced performance. Constant feeding of tit-bits will spoil horses, which will then become disobedient and insubordinate and will constantly try to reverse the pre-eminence of the trainer/rider. Unreasonable and unlimited punishment makes horses frightened and obstinate, and later even vicious and dangerous.

A fundamental mistake frequently made during training is to expect human reactions from a horse. All horses, in common with other animals, will react according to primitive inherited reflexes. Only a trainer who understands basic animal psychology will be successful.

1(2) Psycho-Anatomic Considerations

1(2)i BASIC CONDITIONS

The rider's weight plays an important part in training and riding a horse. Every trainer therefore should be aware of the horse's technique in carrying weight, and of its proportional balance.

Of particular note are the functions of *the back* – especially the neck and back band running from the poll to the sacral vertebrae. On top of the thoracic, lumbar and sacral vertebrae are dorsal fins which up to the fifteenth thoracic vertebrae slant backwards. The sixteenth stands vertically. All the remaining dorsal fins slant forwards towards the head. The spine forms a bridge, with the fore and hind legs as pillars. This construction of the horse's back is therefore designed to carry loads – much more so than the backs of other animals.

Head and neck are supported in their position by the highly elastic band of neck and back muscles. They act as a lever, extending over the supporting forelegs. The carriage of head and neck and the contents of the intestines determine the position of the centre of gravity. When the horse is standing still, its centre of gravity is positioned approximately at the height of the sternum under the centre of the trunk. The position of the centre of gravity is most important in relation to the position of saddle and rider. When the horse is standing still, the centre of gravity is closer to the forehand. The forelegs carry more weight than the hind legs, with approximate distribution of 55% to 45%.

The forelegs carry more weight at halt and in motion, so their function is more that of supporting and braking the horse's weight which is pushed forward from behind.

The hind legs are an acutely angled lever mechanism, capable of activating an enormous propulsive force. The hind legs create the thrust, which is transmitted forward through the spine to be received in the front.

The very different roles of forelegs and hind legs are due to the manner in which these limbs are attached to the body. The hind legs are connected directly to the pelvis/spine bone structure, permitting the transmission of the propulsive power. The free-moving and braking ability of the forelegs, however, depend on the elastic muscular attachment which suspends the ribcage between the shoulder blades.

The neck and back band are a set of muscles extending from the poll to the tail and half way down the hind legs. This band is of tremendous importance in the horse's training, as its degree of tension and contraction determines whether the forward motion (originating in the

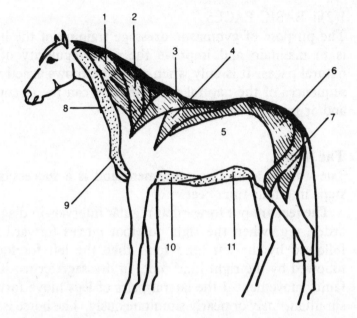

Neck-Back Band
1   Splenius
2,3 Trapezius
4   Latissimus dorsi
5   Lumbodorsal fascia
6   Gluteus
7   Semitendinosus

Throat-Belly Band
8   Brachiocephalicus
9   Biceps brachii
10 M. pectoralis
11 Aponeurosis of oblique
    abdominus extensor

quarters) is transmitted freely with a swinging movement or is strangled by a rigid and tense back muscle.

The young horse contracts the back muscles in response to an unfamiliar weight burden, which causes cramp and stiffness. This applies not only to the initial training of the horse but to the beginning of every training or riding session. Thoughtful training therefore must at all times be concerned with relaxing and gymnastically suppling the neck and back band muscle, allowing the back to swing correctly.

1(2)ii BASIC PACES

The purpose of gymnastic dressage training of the horse is to maintain and improve the even regularity of his natural paces. It is only when a trainer knows exactly the sequences of the natural paces that he can try to correct and/or improve them.

The Walk

The walk is a striding movement and is a succession of steps in a four-time beat.

The feet are put forward at regular intervals in diagonal order, e.g. when the right forefoot moves forward it is followed by the left hind foot, then the left forefoot is followed by the right hind foot. In dressage terms, it is a faulty movement if the lateral pairs of legs move forward simultaneously or nearly simultaneously. The horse is said to be 'pacing' or nearly pacing.

At medium walk the hind feet should reach a little over the imprints of the forefeet.

The Trot

The trot is a *two-time* pace. The feet are moved forward and touch the ground in diagonal pairs. Both diagonals are separated by a moment of suspension, because one diagonal leaves the ground a little before the other touches down.

The Canter

The canter is a *three-time* pace, each canter stride separated from the next one by a moment of suspension. One lateral pair of legs reaches further forward than the other. The leading pair of legs determines if the horse is in right or left canter.

After the moment of suspension the outside hind leg touches down first, followed by the outside diagonal; and lastly the inside forefoot touches down.

Rein-back

The rein-back is not a basic pace as such, but since it is a regular movement sequence it is mentioned here.

It is a two-time (or *almost* two-time) movement. Diagonal pairs of feet are moved backwards and touch the ground simultaneously or almost simultaneously. One diagonal touches down before the other lifts off. In contrast to the trot movement there is therefore no moment of suspension.

The variations within the different paces have already been mentioned in the first part of this book.

Extraordinary Paces

Walk, trot and canter are the basic paces of the riding horse. Inherited or acquired additional paces are the 'Tölt' and the 'Pace'.

The Tölt is a movement at a fast four-time beat, with a high neck carriage. The minimum speed of this pace is 200 metres (220 yds) per minute. Although a 'tölting' horse moves energetically forward with a high knee action, the middle portion of the trunk remains completely still, making it very comfortable to sit to, as it does not bounce the rider.

The Pace is a movement in which the horse moves forward with lateral pairs of legs. This sliding movement (at a fast pace it is even a *floating* movement) is comfortable for the rider to sit to and is sometimes preferred when long distances have to be covered or if the animal is merely a carrier. In most cases the 'Pace' is a trained movement, i.e. an acquired pace.

1(3) The Training Scale

The aim of basic training is to produce a pleasantly moving, obedient, willing, able and skilful riding horse. This is achieved by a systematic training programme,

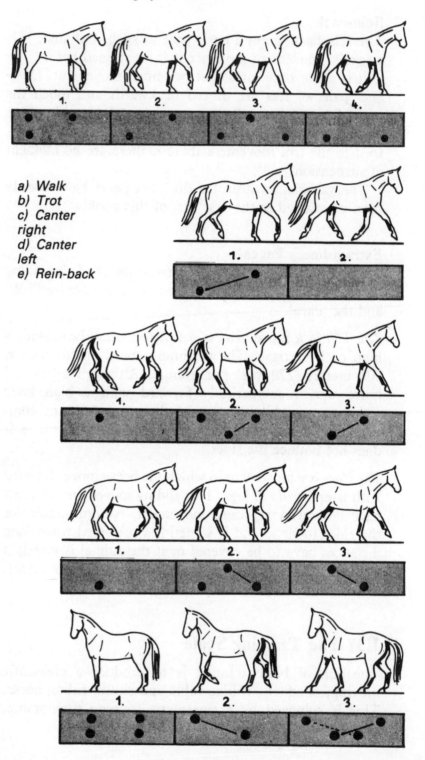

a) Walk
b) Trot
c) Canter right
d) Canter left
e) Rein-back

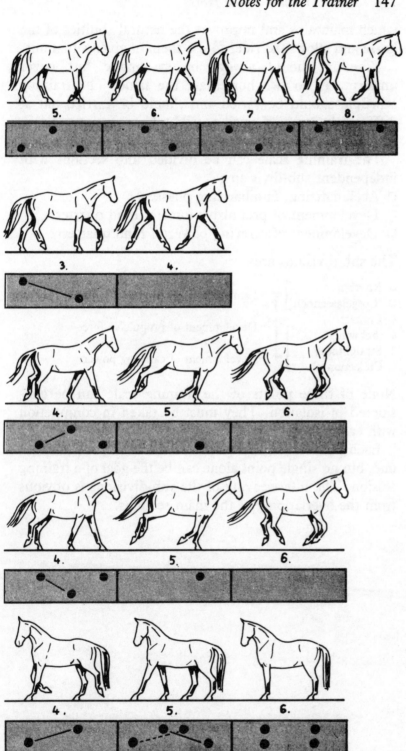

which maintains and improves the natural abilities of the horse and allows the rider to use them in given situations.

Training should always be systematic but never uniform, as no two horses are the same. The training schedule should be varied and should be carried out at different locations if at all possible. Cross-country riding should form a large part of training.

The training scale can be divided into sections with independent sub-divisions:

□ Acclimatizing, familiarizing phase.
□ Development of propulsive force of hind quarters.
□ Development of carrying power of hind quarters.

The sub-divisions are:

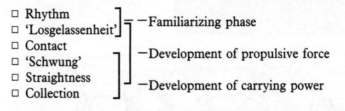

□ Rhythm
□ 'Losgelassenheit' } — Familiarizing phase
□ Contact
□ 'Schwung' } — Development of propulsive force
□ Straightness
□ Collection } — Development of carrying power

None of these points of the training scale can be considered in isolation. They must be taken in conjunction with each other.

Each point is required for the development of the next one, but no single point alone can be the goal of a training session. The interweaving of the sub-divisions is obvious from the overlapping of the main sections.

2. Comprehensive Basic Training

2(1) The Acclimatizing Phase (Backing)

2(1)i INTRODUCING THE HORSE TO THE STABLE, AND TACKING UP

Usually basic training does not take place where the horse was born and reared. The resulting change of surroundings, stabling, and feeding often has a severe impact on the further development of the horse. A patient and understanding trainer will give the young horse time to settle in; this generally takes only a few days but in severe cases can take longer.

Great care must be taken when getting the young horse used to bridle and saddle. This is best done in the familiar surroundings of his stable. The pleasant associations of the stable – comfort and feeding – will help ease his acceptance of strange tack etc. However, putting on a saddle for the first time and tightening the girth should be done in a more spacious area, such as an indoor school, a manège or a spacious yard. Some 'escape' leaps can be expected, not only when saddling up for the first time, but also earlier when the horse will be looking at everything with suspicion. These predictable defence mechanisms can be hazardous and can cause falls, in a box, or particularly on the slippery floor of a passage in stable barns.

When a young horse is tacked up for the first time the trainer will need an assistant; it should not be done by someone on their own. First the horse should be shown the tack and allowed to sniff it. Then the bridle should be put on carefully and slowly. (The correct procedure is explained on pages 35–36 of this book.) Next a numnah is placed across the horse's back, from both sides, and taken off again. Then the numnah and the saddle are lifted on to the back, held there, and taken off again.

The assistant should hold the horse so that he stands relaxed. The saddle can then be lifted on, and the girth carefully tightened. As the girth cannot be tightened very much to begin with, a breast-plate is necessary to keep the saddle in place, in case the horse should jump around. A slipping saddle would frighten him badly.

The assistant holding the horse should have a lunge rein, so that if the horse gives a sudden jump he can remain in control. A horse who gets away in the initial stages of training will take a long time to settle before he stands still to be tacked up again.

2(1)ii LUNGEING

Lungeing a horse in preparation for training under the rider is helpful – in many cases necessary. The young horse will thus get used to working, will learn to obey, and will start to become flexible and agile. During further training you can always return to lungeing if incorrect riding has made the horse develop irregularities in pace and/or posture.

Lungeing is especially beneficial for horses with ewe necks and dropped backs. A horse with a short, tense back who finds it hard to relax under the rider may be lunged before being ridden, as a little lateral flexion will

Lungeing

help to relax the spine. Lungeing is also beneficial to horses which after a lay-off are only allowed to do light work.

Lungeing ring

Lungeing should be carried out in a quiet spot, where the going is not too deep. Any outside distraction devalues work on the lunge, which is why it should not take place in a manège where horses are being schooled; the other horses could also be side-tracked by the lunge horse.

A surrounding fence or barrier will guide the horse on the circle and prevent him from trying to escape. In a manège it is easy to construct a lungeing ring, either from straw bales, barrels with poles, or wings. Stud farms or riding schools which practise lungeing regularly often have a permanent lungeing ring, sometimes even a covered one.

Equipment

The horse should be tacked up with bridle and saddle. With young horses, and also when doing collected work

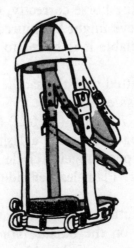

Cavesson   *Lungeing roller*

**Horse tacked up
for lungeing**

*With cavesson
over the bridle*

*Lunge-rein attached to
a leather coupling
between the two bit rings*

in advanced training, a cavesson should be used for lungeing. It must be adjusted to fit the horse correctly, otherwise there is a danger that his eye might be injured. If a
well-fitting cavesson is not available it is better to lunge
off a snaffle bridle.

A lungeing roller should be fitted over the saddle, with
rings on both sides to take the side reins.

Also needed are a lunge line 7 metres (23 feet) (minimum) in length and a lungeing whip with a lash long
enough to reach the horse easily on a lungeing circle 12–14
metres (39–46 feet) in diameter. Plain leather side reins
should be used.

Standing martingales and other equipment which
neither give the horse support on the outside nor limit
the amount of bend in the neck are not advisable, as they
allow the horse to overbend and to go crooked. The
horse's legs should also be protected.

Adjusting Side Reins and Lunge

At first the young horse should be lunged without any auxiliary reins. Later on, side reins of equal length should be used. They should be attached to the lungeing roller, level with the point of the horse's shoulder. They must be adjusted so that the horse is able to lengthen his neck forwards/downwards, with his nasal bone always in front of the vertical.

With spoiled horses the side reins should be adjusted according to the purpose of the lungeing. For a horse who carries his head and neck too high, the side reins should be adjusted to a slightly higher ring. For a horse carrying his head and neck too low, the side reins should be attached lower. Later on, when practising collected work on the lunge, the side reins should be adjusted higher according to requirement.

However, lungeing will only be successful if the forward driving aids of the lunge whip are used as necessary.

Under no circumstances should the side reins be adjusted too tightly. This causes resistance in the mouth and back, which develops the underneck muscles and, in conjunction with the tension and stiffness in the back, also tightens the shoulders and makes the paces tense.

The extent to which the side reins are used to bend the horse on the curve of the circle depends on the stage of training. When lungeing correctly it is mainly the lunge line which guides the horse on the circle and bends it according to the circle curvature. At the same time the horse must be able to lean against the outside side rein. As a rule it is therefore correct to have the side reins at equal lengths, or to shorten the inside side rein only slightly in comparison to the outside one.

If lungeing with a cavesson, the lunge should be attached to the inside ring. Only when extra power is needed should it be attached to the centre ring. If the lunge has a buckle, the tongue should point away from the horse.

When lungeing with a bridle and side reins, the lunge

should be attached to the inside bit-ring. Without side reins (i.e. with a young horse), and if no cavesson is available, the lunge should be attached to a leather coupling between the two bit-rings. This prevents the bit from being pulled through the horse's mouth, should it suddenly jerk away.

In advanced training when working for collection, the lunge may be threaded through the inside bit-ring over the poll and attached to the outside bit-ring. This method of attaching the lunge requires a high degree of feel in the hand and is not recommended for novice training. Neither is it recommended for basic training.

The Technique of Lungeing

Generally, lungeing is started on the left-hand rein. The trainer will bring a schooled horse into the centre of the circle to begin the session. With the left hand he holds the lunge in equal, neat loops. With the whip held in his right hand he lightly touches the horse's left hock, causing it to move forward. Then letting the lunge slip gently through his hand while pushing the horse with the whip, he guides the horse in walk on to the perimeter of the circle.

When on the left rein the lunge should always be carried in the left hand, and vice versa. The thumb, pressed down on to the second joint of the index finger, should keep the lunge firmly in the trainer's hand. There should always be one loop left in the hand, to allow for a little 'give' in case the horse should suddenly jump.

Once the horse is on the track the trainer should stay in a spot in the centre, turning with the speed of the horse. The hand holding the lunge should be held at approximately the height of the horse's mouth, with the elbow held lightly by the side of the body. The lunge must have a light but steady contact with the mouth. The lunge whip should be held in the other hand, creating the necessary forward impulsion. It should point towards the

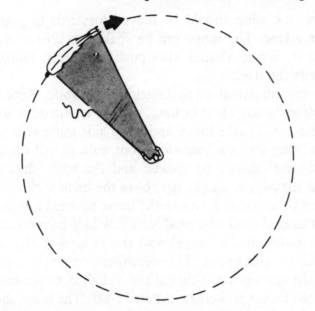

Position of the trainer in the centre of the circle

horse's inside hock. This way the horse is 'framed' between the lunge and the whip.

To use the lunge whip, the trainer's hand should describe a small circle from above downwards, from below upwards, and at the same time from behind forward. This movement flicks the lash from below upwards. To gain the horse's respect the end of the lash should now and again touch him just above the hock.

If the horse has a tendency to decrease the circle and

fall in, the whip should be moved forwards to point to his shoulder. The lunge can be shaken to create 'waves' along it, which should also push the horse more out towards the track.

A very influential aid in lungeing is the voice. Repeating the same signals, short or long, with an energetic or soothing tone, will make lunge and whip aids more effective.

To bring about a transition from walk to trot the command 'trot' should be spoken and the whip should be raised slightly; or a light tap above the hock with the lash should be applied. To make the horse proceed into canter the trainer should first produce a few half-halts (repeated slight pulls on the lunge) and the strides of the horse should be shortened. The command 'canter', together with the appropriate whip aid and a slightly firmer contact with the mouth will create the strike-off. The horse should never break into canter out of an increasingly faster trot. A horse who has been well schooled on the lunge quickly learns a canter strike-off from a walk, urged by the word 'canter' together with a slight raising of the whip.

To make a downward transition one again relies on the voice. The slowly enunciated command 'ter-rot' in a diminishing tone, accompanied by repeated slight pulls on the lunge will make the horse change to trot. The same falling intonation in the command 'wa-a-lk' should be used for the transition to walk. Only when the horse is in the new pace should the whip be used again to maintain impulsion.

Once the horse is on the track he should stay there. Even to change rein he must be halted on the track. The trainer should then approach the horse, gathering the lunge in equal loops. The horse can be turned with the whip, as in a turn around the forehand.

The whip should never be put down on the ground; whenever the trainer has to adjust the side reins on the girth, etc. he should hold it under his armpit. Picking up the whip from the ground might easily frighten the horse; also he might accidentally stand on the whip.

The lungeing should start and end with the walk. During the final walk the side reins should be loosened considerably or taken off altogether. In general it can be said that, while lungeing, the pace has to be changed often; also the rein should be changed regularly. Both will increase the suppleness and relaxation of the back muscles – which is the ultimate aim of lunge training.

Lungeing a young horse
Lungeing a young horse should be carried out by two people: the trainer and a helper. The trainer should stay in the centre and apply the aids as described for the schooled horse. At the same time the helper should lead the young horse out to the track and should then walk by its head, around the circle.

When the horse seems happy enough to walk along the track, the helper can return to the trainer or, may, perhaps, take the whip and follow the horse close to its quarters, inside the circle.

It is important for this work to be carried out in a positive manner, but with patience and calmness. Very soon the horse will understand the meaning of lunge, whip, and voice, and will go willingly on the lunge on both reins. Work on the lunge should not exceed thirty minutes; with young horses it should be twenty minutes. It should contain many changes of rein and a great deal of praise for the horse.

2(1)iii BACKING AND PRELIMINARY EXERCISES UNDER SADDLE
While in his box and during grooming, the young horse will become accustomed to being handled. The groom should pat him all over and occasionally lean carefully across his withers.

Mounting a horse for the first time should be accomplished very carefully, quietly, and in a relaxed way. Even the most placid horse may get frightened when a rider suddenly sits on his back. Again, the first impression is a lasting one.

The trainer will decide where and when the horse is to be mounted for the first time. As a rule it should be done in a spacious enclosure, such as an indoor school or a manège. The horse should be held by an assistant while the rider is slowly lifted up. At first he should only lean across the withers or saddle, but when crossing his leg over for the first time he has to be very agile, so as not to make any unnecessary movements, and to avoid touching the horse's croup. He will then slide gently into the saddle, at first keeping his upper body in a crouching position, then straightening up gradually and slowly. Constant patting and talking to the horse, as well as offering a few tit-bits, will distract his attention from what is happening on his back. The assistant should ease the rider into the stirrups. In case the horse should plunge a little, the rider can take hold of a neckstrap. Under no circumstances should he balance himself with the reins.

When the horse moves off, led by the assistant, the rider should follow his movement passively. Later the helper should walk by the horse's head, without actually holding it, but ready to assist if necessary.

These initial riding sessions should not take long, but the horse must learn to carry the rider calmly – initially only at walk, but later on for a few strides at trot. At the end of the session the rider should dismount equally carefully, then should be lifted up again a couple of times. Depending on the horse's performance, the rider can soon start to mount with the foot in the stirrup. If time is available, this short riding session should be repeated the same day. It will speed up the horse's progress considerably.

Another important requisite in the preliminary lungeing and riding period is that all tack should fit correctly. A young horse is not fully developed in its contours, and the saddle might easily slip. The horse must therefore be re-saddled frequently; simply tightening the girth is not

Riding a young
horse with one
or two lead
horses

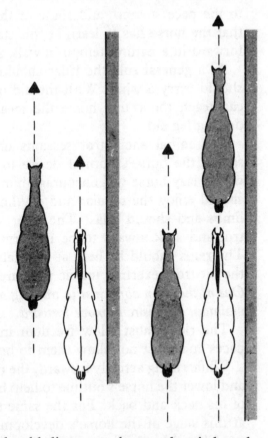

enough. The rider should dismount, loosen the girth and
lift the saddle backwards into its original position. This
will give the horse's back a welcome relief from the rider's
weight. A fore-girth might also be of help in keeping the
saddle in place. After riding, the young horse's tender
skin in the girth area and under the seat of the saddle must
be attended to, and possibly hardened off with methylated
spirits.

This preliminary training under the rider can be greatly
simplified if the young horse can be ridden in company
with others. A reliable lead-horse should be used alongside and a little in front of the young horse. If two lead-
horses are available, one should be used directly in front,
and the other alongside the young horse. The animal then
has no escape route, and in the 'herd' it will quickly adapt

to the pace, tempo, and route of the other animals. All that the horse has to learn at this stage is to move freely forward in a natural tempo in walk and trot.

As a general rule the rider should not wear spurs but should carry a whip. With the aid of whip and voice he can teach the young horse the meaning of the forward driving leg aid.

The initial short trot sessions on both reins should satisfy the horse's natural desire to move forward; and with a lazy horse will encourage him to do so. The horse should enjoy the regular and rhythmic movement of his limbs and should relax. The rider should ride in rising trot and seek always to be in harmony with the horse. The reins should be held at a suitable length to prevent the bit from exerting undue pressure on the bars.

One of the main objectives in training a horse is to create and maintain his desire to move forward.

The rider must allow freedom in the horse's natural paces and must not allow them to become shorter.

While riding actively forward, the rider should lengthen and lower the horse's outline to help him relax the muscles of his neck and back. For the same reason it is vital that at this stage of the horse's development the rider should not 'shape' his outline with the reins.

Riding forward, however, does not mean over-riding the pace or allowing the young horse to run off. If the horse offers to canter, the rider should allow him to do so. In canter the rider should sit light, with deep hands (but not pressing them down). Thus the horse can canter with ease and can round his back. The canter should only be performed for short periods. Otherwise the horse will come too much on to the forehand and the rider's hand.

During exercise the young horse needs rest periods. These can be utilized to teach him various aspects of obedience: halting in a relaxed way, in any direction; mounting; dismounting; and re-saddling; during all of which the horse has to learn to stand immobile.

General thoughts on the backing of young horses
☐ Young horses, especially those with weak backs, should be ridden only by light riders. This is important – at least until the back muscles are well developed. During the initial training period all young horses become stiff (muscle-bound) which will show in stiff movements.
☐ The rider should mount quietly, follow the horse's movement gently, and ride in a light seat position. Every sudden or harsh thrust on the horse's back will cause tenseness of the back muscles.
☐ Under the rider's weight the inborn rhythmic, springy and ground-covering movement of the young horse must be maintained. Every time that the rider mounts a young horse the back muscles will tense up against him. So each time after mounting, the rider must relax these muscles with suppling and loosening exercises.

Once a young horse relaxes the muscles of his neck and back band he will walk on a loose rein with a long, low outline, stretching his nose confidently forwards/downwards. The back will swing with the walk, and the tail will swing like a pendulum from side to side. The horse will be over-tracking with regular steps and engaged quarters.

This stage of training has to be achieved FIRST, before riding the horse forward into a light contact in trot, canter and later in walk, to begin shaping his outline.

2(2) Developing the Propulsive Force of the Quarters

2(2)i RHYTHM

After approximately one month the young horse will be used to the rider's weight on his back, and his training can progress.

The next step is to establish rhythm by maintaining a certain tempo suited to the horse's own natural basic pace.

To achieve this the rider must ride the horse forward evenly, with an elastic but still and deep hand.

'Forward' does not mean 'faster'. In a faster tempo the horse would be running and would break his rhythm. 'Forward' means engaging the quarters and asking the hind legs to actively propel the horse's body forward.

The regularity of movement in all three paces is the foremost objective in this phase of training.

2(2)ii LOSGELASSENHEIT

The German term 'Losgelassenheit' can be interpreted as suppleness combined with looseness and with a complete absence of any tension – i.e. the horse is unconstrained.

A correct rhythm can be achieved only if the horse's back is swinging. The muscles of the neck and back band must not only be relaxed, but must work and swing with the movement of the horse's legs.

All joints should bend and stretch equally well, and the horse's whole body must convey the impression of looseness and suppleness in all joints, as well as willingness to co-operate and to move actively forward. Without the willingness of the horse there cannot be true *Losgelassenheit*.

Indications of *Losgelassenheit* are:

☐ A content and happy expression (eye, ears).
☐ Tail carried and swinging like a pendulum with the horse's movement.
☐ A rhythmically swinging back (rider able to sit).
☐ Horse champing the bit lightly with *closed* mouth. (Relaxing the neck muscles opens the exit channels of the parotid glands: saliva is produced; the chewing and swallowing movement produces the foam at the edge of the horse's mouth.)
☐ A purring rhythmic 'snort' or 'blowing', which is a sign that the horse is mentally relaxed.

Losgelassenheit is achieved if the young horse moves naturally and rhythmically forward in all three paces, with his neck lowered forwards/downwards and with his back swinging. The horse should now accept the forward driving aids without rushing, and the rider is able to push.

2(2)iii CONTACT

Closely connected with the development of rhythm and *Losgelassenheit* is the establishment of a steady contact. It gives the horse the necessary confidence to re-balance himself under the additional weight of the rider, and to find the rhythm of the various paces.

Contact is a soft and steady connection between the rider's hand and the horse's mouth. While training progresses, the horse should be ridden more from behind into the elastically yielding hand. The contact will then be even on both reins when riding straight ahead, and a little stronger on the outside rein when riding on a circle.

To achieve a contact the reins may not be moved backwards. Contact has to be the result of well-developed propulsive power. When forward driving aids are applied *the horse has to move forward into the contact.*

When ridden on a contact the horse's outline is determined by his balance. At first he will carry his neck rather low and his mouth in line with the point of his shoulder, to allow the neck and back band muscle to relax and stretch.

Contact does not mean that the horse may lie on the rider's hand. He must find his own balance and not try to use the reins as a 'fifth leg'. Should he try to do so, the rider must counteract it with energetic forward driving aids and a yielding rein.

To establish a contact the rider must bring the horse's hind legs further underneath his body. This stretches and elasticates the neck and back band muscles. The rider can feel clearly in both hands and under his seat how the forehand and quarters are connected by the back muscle. He can feel how the activity of the quarters causes the

The Horse's Outline

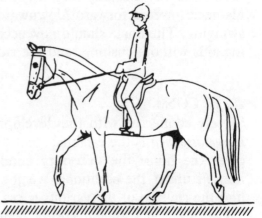

On the bit

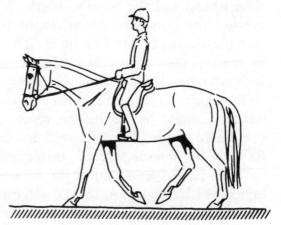

On a long rein

On a loose rein

back to swing with suppleness and elasticity, resulting in calm and regular strides.

Through this swinging back the propulsive force generated by the quarters can now be transmitted forward to the horse's mouth. The horse submits to the energy coming from behind: he flexes in the poll and champs the bit – in other words he is *on the bit*. This situation also provides an opportunity to influence the hind quarters with the reins.

When a horse is on the bit the poll is always the highest point, with the nasal bone just in front of the vertical. The curvature and length of the horse's neck depend on the activity of the hind legs. They must never be determined by the hand alone.

At this stage of schooling the young horse when in walk may only be ridden on a long rein, i.e. with a long neck but on a light contact. If the slight contact is lost (with the rider carrying the reins at the buckle) the horse is 'on a loose rein'. This is done at walk only, during a break in work, or as a reward after a working session.

When establishing a contact with the horse's mouth, many riders make the following mistakes:

☐ *FALSE BEND* The contact was established with the rein action only. The highest point is no longer the poll, but lies between the third and fourth vertebrae.

This is a serious mistake. It can only be corrected – if at all – through long-lasting and thorough training. It is important that while riding energetically forward the rider's hands should be able to restrain the horse from rushing or losing his rhythm. On the other hand they must yield sufficiently to allow the horse to lengthen his neck, to remedy the false bend and exchange it for a flexion at the poll.

☐ *BEHIND THE VERTICAL* This fault also originates from too much rein action. It often occurs together with a false bend. Yielding the reins and energetic riding forward are the remedy.

□ *BEHIND THE BIT* Here the horse goes with a false bend and behind the vertical, but he also tries not to accept the bit by creeping behind it, escaping backwards.

In this case, contact must be established with the mouth. The horse must learn to accept the hand. This fault often means going back a long way in the training programme, to the time when the horse was being ridden on a long rein.

Lungeing with long side reins can often help.

After a contact with the mouth has been established, the horse is corrected forward, as with the last two faults. Here the forward riding should be in canter, preferably out of doors and across country, encouraging the horse to stretch his nose forwards/downwards into the contact.

Another mistake which riders make, especially when trying to correct the above faults, is holding their hands too high. This, of course, has a negative effect, because to try to get the horse to stretch its nose forwards/downwards the rider's hands have to move in the same direction – i.e. 'pushing' the horse's nose forwards/downwards.

□ *AGAINST/ABOVE THE BIT* When the horse does not 'give' in the poll, he develops a ewe neck, and the dropped back is tense and stiff. He goes *against* the rider's hand, with the nasal bone well in front of the vertical. To correct this, the horse has to be worked a lot on circles and large serpentines to make him supple and to bend him laterally. Lungeing with deeper and longer than normal side reins is helpful.

Holding the hands extremely deep or pulling backwards on the reins are serious mistakes. A horse's head *cannot be and should not be* pulled downwards.

*Lengthening the horse's neck when asking
him to champ the reins out of the rider's hands*

2(2)iv TESTING RHYTHM, 'LOSGELASSENHEIT' AND CONTACT

In order to test if these three aims have been achieved successfully, an exercise known as *allowing the horse to champ the reins out of the rider's hands* can be used.

In this exercise, again, the forward driving aids are extremely important. Rhythm and tempo have to remain the same, before, during and after the exercise. The horse should be ridden forward and then allowed to champ the reins out of the rider's hands. His nose should move forwards/downwards, his neck should be rounded, and he should walk in a relaxed way. He must neither hurry nor slow down.

In this exercise the rein should only be yielded to the length of a 'long rein' (not given altogether), at which point the horse should again feel contact with the rider's hand. Generally speaking, this would be when the horse's mouth is level with the point of his shoulder.

If the horse does not want to lengthen his outline when the reins are yielded, or if he jerks the reins out of the rider's hands, it is a sign that his neck and back muscles are not yet supple enough. It is nearly always caused by the rider using too much rein and not enough leg aid.

This testing exercise of yielding the reins can be done at any pace. After the exercise, the reins should be shortened again, or, in walk, dropped altogether. An excellent use of the exercise is to carry it out repeatedly in canter on a large circle. Each time the reins are shortened it must be done very gently and smoothly, inch by inch, without disturbing the mouth.

2(2)v 'SCHWUNG'

'Schwung' is the transmission of the energetic impulse created by the hind legs, into the forward movement of the entire horse. An elastically swinging back is the necessary pre-condition.

'Schwung' should not merely be interpreted as impulsion. A horse can show impulsion – e.g. a racehorse – and not have 'Schwung'.

'Schwung' is not identified by the horse being a 'good' or 'showy' mover. A horse can be born with a good trot, showing long, extended steps. But this natural action can easily be performed in a tense way, with a rigid back and high head carriage.

'Schwung' is always the result of efficient training, which uses the natural pace but adds to it the horse's suppleness, looseness, elasticity, and responsiveness to the aids.

'Schwung' can be recognized by the fact that immediately after the foot pushes off the ground, the hock is energetically bent in a forward direction, and not first pulled upwards or even backwards. The back muscles absorb this impulsive, bouncy movement, and allow the rider to sit comfortably, swinging with the movement. In most cases the development of 'Schwung' also produces improved action of the forelimbs.

'Schwung' can exist only in trot and canter, as only these two paces have a moment of suspension (not in walk). The moment of suspension is the critical moment which shows if a pace has 'Schwung' or not. The more pronounced the moment of suspension, the more 'Schwung' a horse has. With 'Schwung' he will cover more ground in extended paces and the working and collected paces will be more pronounced. 'Schwung' therefore can be developed in the working and collected paces as well as in medium and extended trot or canter.

2(2)vi PRINCIPLES FOR THE DEVELOPMENT OF THE PROPULSIVE FORCE

Development in Trot
The working trot with its controllable two-time diagonal beat is the most suitable pace for effecting improvement of rhythm, *Losgelassenheit*, contact and 'Schwung'.

By means of forward driving aids and FEEL for the movement of the individual horse, the rider has to find out and maintain his typical working trot. Since each horse has an ideal tempo for his different pace and length of stride there is no set rule for measuring the working trot. The only guideline would be that the hind feet should reach at least the imprints of the forefeet.

The working trot is the primary pace from which to develop propulsive force, necessary for medium and collected trot. With increased forward driving aids and a definite contact the trot strides should be lengthened. At first, only a few strides are required, which will with progressive training develop into medium trot.

It is important for the gymnastic development of the horse that the downward transitions to working trot should be smooth and submissive. Then, later on, through a shortened trot, a good transition can be made to collected trot.

Development in Canter
A good working trot is the foundation of a good canter. As soon as the young horse has learned to relax his back and is able to carry the rider in balance through shallow

turns (corners in a school, rounded off), work in canter can be started.

The rider should proceed from working trot to canter as described in Section I of this book. If the young horse tries to increase the tempo before strike-off, the rider has first to slow him down and then should repeat the canter aid.

Some young horses have weak backs and poorly muscled quarters, and they therefore find it hard to strike-off in canter – which would mean having to arch their back under the rider's additional weight. To ease the burden, the rider should keep his hips well forward but should lean his upper body a little forward as well. At first the horse should also be allowed to take a little stronger contact with a low neck carriage. Later on, when the horse's back has become stronger and his quarters better muscled, the rider will be able to straighten up, and by riding more forward will lighten the contact to a normal and desirable degree.

Cantering for short periods only and repeating the transition to canter will often teach the horse to pick the correct lead easily, and in time an even and regular work-

Outline of a young horse when cantering

ing canter will be established. The rider must work for and maintain a natural calm stride.

The medium canter is the pace which best improves the horse's propulsive force. It also improves *Losgelassenheit*. Practised out of doors on long lines it is developed gradually by increasingly engaging the horse's quarters while allowing the hands to move forward in rhythm with the stride.

Development in Walk

A calm walk covering plenty of ground is an important pace for any horse. A horse with a short walk, rushing and continuously breaking into trot, is in most cases of a nervous disposition and is most uncomfortable to sit on.

To maintain a good natural walk, to improve a poor walk, or to lengthen the walk steps, the rider should sit quietly, allow the natural nodding movement of the horse's head and neck while maintaining an even and steady contact. His lower legs must be in constant contact with the horse's sides, increasing calf pressure on alternate sides the moment each hind leg is brought forward.

Outline of a young horse when walking on a light contact

172 Basic Training of the Horse

If the horse is not attentive or is very lazy, the leg aid should be supported by spurs and whip.

The young horse should be ridden at walk with long reins until the walk is calm, free and rhythmic. Only then can the rider take up a very light contact. Only after one and a half years may the horse be asked to walk on the bit.

The walk is the one pace in which rhythm and freedom of movement can be most easily spoiled by bad riding.

Many riders spoil the rhythm and freedom of the walk by using rest periods (in walk) to shape their horse's outline with the reins.

Another way in which the natural walk is interfered with and the rhythm damaged is if the rider does not follow the movement with his hands, but keeps them still, impairing the natural nodding movement, and therefore the natural balance of the walk.

It is not only bad hands which disturb the walk. The same damage can be inflicted by incorrect use of leg aids. Horses become lazy in walk and 'dead' to the leg aid if the rider's leg constantly presses or kicks.

With both highly-strung and sensible horses it is usual for inexperienced riders to take their leg off the horse so as not to further upset him. This, however, only succeeds in making the rider's seat loose and the horse flighty. With such horses it is essential for the rider's lower leg to be in constant contact with the horse's sides. The sensitive horse will quickly learn to accept the leg contact and will settle into a calm, relaxed walk. Only at this point will the rider be able to improve the walk by alternate leg aids.

2(3) Development of the Hind Quarters

2(3)i STRAIGHTENING THE HORSE
The horse's propulsive force, developed by the quarters, can only be fully utilized in forward direction if the horse

Natural crookedness
and straightening
of the
young horse

Shoulder fore

Riding in position

Crooked horse
(to the right)

174 Basic Training of the Horse

moves 'straight'. A horse is 'straight' if the hind feet follow exactly the same line as the front feet. Only then can the rider transfer more weight evenly on to both hind legs increasing their carrying power. Most horses' bodies are naturally crooked. This is even more pronounced because a horse is narrower in his shoulders than in his hips. Most horses move with their right hind leg outside alongside the track of the right front leg. The propulsive force of this right hind leg moves diagonally across to the horse's left shoulder, transferring additional weight on to the left front leg and giving the rider a much stronger contact on the left rein. In this case the horse will also lean against the rider's right leg.

Occasionally a horse is crooked in the other direction, with corresponding results on the other side.

To straighten a horse his forehand has to be brought squarely in front of his quarters. Logically, the forehand must be aligned with the quarters, and not vice versa, as it is in the quarters that all forward movement originates.

When a horse is straightened his spine is always shaped according to the line he is moving on, be this on a straight line or on a circle.

If a horse is crooked to the right – e.g. right hind leg outside the track of right front leg – the rider, with his right leg and rein, must inhibit any further sideways deviation of the right hind leg. He should apply his left leg closer to the girth, causing the horse's left hind leg to reach further forward. He should support with the left rein held low, against the horse's left shoulder, and guide the forehand with the right rein towards the right, until the horse's right front leg moves straight in front of the right hind leg.

The rider should begin to straighten a horse the moment that he starts listening to the aids. But specialized straightening training can only begin with the development of propulsive force and 'Schwung', because in straightening, the horse has to be ridden forward with determination. (Of course, this does not mean more speed but increased activity of the quarters.)

Exercises to straighten a horse are:

In preliminary training
□ Riding on circles.
□ Leg-yielding in a slow trot.

In more advanced training
□ Riding lateral movements such as 'shoulder-in'.

As preparation for 'shoulder-in', preliminary forms of the movement are ridden – one being riding a horse 'in position'. From this develops the movement 'shoulder fore', which in turn evolves into 'shoulder-in'. All stages help to straighten a horse, and the preliminary ones can be ridden in basic training.

When ridden 'in position' the horse is very slightly bent laterally, in an even line from head to tail. The horse's foreleg should be brought in front of the inside hind leg, the forehand remaining on the track. The horse's outside hind foot should now step straight forward in the direction of the outside shoulder, while the inside hind foot should be made to step not only forward but also a little in the direction between the forelegs.

This position is developed into 'shoulder fore', where the forehand is taken a little into the school, so that the outside hind foot still moves towards the outside shoulder, but the inside hind foot, viewed from the front, steps clearly between the front legs.

By bringing the forehand even more in from the track, and with increased collection, 'shoulder-in' is developed.

2(3)ii COLLECTION

The aim of all gymnastic training is to create a useful horse which is willing to perform.

The deciding factor here is that the horse's and the rider's weight are distributed evenly over all four legs. To achieve this, the carrying power of the hind legs has to be increased. The front legs, whose original function was of a 'supporting and braking' nature, carried most of the weight. Their burden has to be reduced, whereas the hind legs, which by nature have a predominantly pushing role, must now take up some of the weight-carrying task of the front legs.

To achieve this change, the propulsive force should be increased by stronger forward driving aids, but should now not be let out forward – as for example when lengthening the stride by yielding the reins. It is now received and caught by the reins with a non-allowing or even a regulating rein aid – and then returned to the quarters via a supple back. In this way the propulsive power of the hind legs is transformed into carrying power.

Two factors make this transformation possible:
☐ The horse must be straight.
☐ The haunches must be well bent and lowered.

A more acute bend of the hind legs involves the centre of gravity being shifted further backwards. The bend of the hind legs, however, depends on the degree of bend of the hip and stifle joint, higher up in the hind leg, which in riding terminology is referred to as 'the haunches'. All joints of the hind leg are inter-related and complementary to one another. Therefore any increased bending of the haunches automatically involves a more acute bending of the other joints lower down the leg.

More acute bending with the increased weight-carrying capacity of the hind legs lowers the quarters. This involves easing the weight on the forehand, which gives greater mobility to the forelegs.

A collected horse gives the onlooker the impression that it is moving 'uphill'. The steps and strides are shorter; and 'Schwung', energy, and activity are sustained, making the horse's movement appear proud and elevated.

The arching of the neck is directly related to the degree of collection. A horse on the bit carrying the normal amount of weight on the quarters moves with a moderately arched and fairly long neck. A collected horse, carrying more weight on the quarters and accordingly less weight on the forehand, moves with a more acutely arched and shorter neck.

When the horse is correctly trained, his neck shapes itself. The lowering of the quarters determines how high the neck is carried and arched; the horse *carries itself*. Whereas if the head and neck position are created by the reins mainly or solely, the rider has to carry the horse's head and neck with his hands.

If the carrying capacity of the quarters is developed sufficiently, the horse is able to carry his own and his rider's weight in perfect balance.

To examine whether a horse is in balance or not, the rider can be asked to 'give and retake' the reins, as is done in some dressage tests. Then, for a few strides, the rider has to give up the contact, which anyway at this stage of training is only light. Momentarily without any contact, a balanced horse will not change tempo nor change his head and neck carriage. This is in contrast to the exercise described earlier, where the young horse, given the reins, follows them by lowering his head and lengthening his neck.

2(3)iii PRINCIPLES OF DEVELOPING THE CARRYING CAPACITY OF THE QUARTERS

In general it can be said that the carrying capacity of the quarters can only be developed after their propulsive force has been established. The rhythm in all three paces has to be established simultaneously, maintaining *Losgelassenheit* and contact. The development of 'Schwung' concerns both the propulsive force and the carrying capacity of the quarters.

There is a saying in German: 'Ride your horse forward and straighten it.' This emphasizes that first and foremost the horse must be ridden forward. The rider must always remember that between and after collecting and straightening exercises he must ride actively forward. Another axiom is: 'The quality of the medium trot is an indicator of the horse's training.' The quality and regularity of a medium trot after work in collection will demonstrate how effective and correctly the collection was executed. If in this medium trot the horse seeks the support of the rider's hand, or if he loses rhythm or stiffens, leaning on one side against the rider's leg, it means that the preceding collected work was overdone or incorrectly executed. However, if the medium trot is produced with regular, pronounced strides; if the horse takes the rider forward with his back swinging, and if he lengthens his outline, it means that the preceding work was correctly executed according to the increased lengthening of strides. The horse must move straight forward with 'Schwung', rhythmically and relaxed, on a light contact.

2(3)iv 'DURCHLAESSIGKEIT'

This is a very important factor in basic training for which there is no equivalent word in English. It describes the horse's immediate willingness to obey the rider's aids without the slightest resistance. To achieve 'Durchlaessigkeit' the horse first has to be 'lossgelassen' – that is, supple and loose throughout his body, so that he is relaxed enough to 'let the rider's aids through'. 'Durchlaessigkeit' can be developed by logical and gymnastic training.

The more the 'Durchlaessigkeit' is improved the quicker the horse will respond to more and more delicately applied aids. This will become most obvious in transitions and halts.

The degree to which 'Durchlaessigkeit' exists in a horse is the measure of the correctness with which the training programme has been applied.

2(4) Exercises for Basic Training

The following exercises are the most useful ones in the basic training of the horse. In each one of these exercises all the various sections of the *Training Scale* concerning a horse at this level have to be considered. The various sections or points of the Training Scale could also be considered as 'basic qualities' of a trained horse.

Therefore the purpose mentioned for each of the following exercises is not to be taken as the sole purpose. It has to be considered in context with the other sections of the Training Scale.

How to ride the various exercises is explained earlier in this book. Therefore only very important points are repeated here. The same applies to the section *Most Common Faults*, which obviously has to be selective.

There is no rigid order in which these exercises can be taught, but it must be progressive. A new exercise should be started only after the previous one has been performed satisfactorily. The various sections of the Training Scale and their inter-dependence on one another should be borne in mind at all times. In each training session horse and rider should have a new objective to aim for.

Training a horse without a systematic programme of well-defined objectives is most unsatisfactory. Without constantly striving for improvement it is inevitable that the horse's existing standard will deteriorate.

Exercise	Purpose of Exercise	Tips for Execution of Exercise	Most Common Faults
Proceed in walk. Medium walk on a long rein.	Accustoming horse to rider's weight. Relaxation. Making horse supple.	Relaxed approach, but energetically forward from the beginning.	Reins too short, 'dead' or regulating hands. Either weak or too much forward driving. Too little time.
Working trot. Rising trot. Circles. Large serpentines. Loops on the long side. Various ways of changing rein.	Rhythm, *Losgelassenheit*, contact, 'Schwung'.	Even tempo with 'Schwung', on straight lines. Even contact on both reins. On circles, pushing more into outside rein. Increased use of outside aids.	Tempo too dull or running. Break in rhythm, especially at corners. Quarters falling out in circles.
Lengthened strides.	Rhythm, 'Schwung'.	Transitions not to be rushed. Important to maintain rhythm.	Transitions too sudden or without energy. Running.
Transitions: working trot-working canter-working trot.	*Losgelassenheit*.	More 'into outside rein', especially on circles. Frequent transitions.	Weak or too sudden aids. Individual sessions too long.

Lengthened strides from working canter	*Losgelassenheit*, 'Schwung'.	Especially on circle: if using full school, important to align forehand with quarters. Maintaining perfect rhythm.	Blurred or too sudden transition. Strides running. Quarters falling in.
Frequent changes of rein.	Intensive suppling effect by working both sides alternatively.	Good figures.	
Transitions: working canter-working trot-walk.	In preliminary stages, suppling. Later, collecting.	Prepare transitions carefully. Downward transitions with forward driving aids. Ease contact after transition to walk.	Not enough preparation for transitions. Transitions on forehand. After transition, not enough forward reins. Too short in walk.
Leg-yielding in walk. Suppleness, looseness, rhythm.	*Losgelassenheit*, rhythm.	Keep neck straight in front of shoulders.	Too much bend in neck. Too little support with outside aids. Running. Sessions too long.

Exercise	Purpose of Exercise	Tips for Execution of Exercise	Most Common Faults
Leg-yielding in trot.	*Losgelassenheit*, straightness.	Shorten working trot.	Too fast. Too small an angle. Too much bend in neck. Too much sideways instead of forward/sideways.
Line-to-line leg-yielding in walk and trot.	At preliminary stage, suppling. Later, collection.	Definite straightening of neck in front of shoulders. Quarters must not lead forehand.	Too little lateral flexion in poll. Too much sideways instead of forward/sideways.
Half-halts.	Alerting horse. Preparation. Improving paces. Collection.	Co-ordination of all aids. Important for forward driving aids to be dominant.	Rein action only. Getting 'stuck' in half-halt because reins did not yield afterwards.
Full halts.	Halting horse. Collection.	Don't forget preparation, with several half-halts.	Lacking preparation. Too much rein action.

Halt. Immobility.	Obedience.	Balanced halt on all four legs.	Lacking practice, therefore immobility not good. Uneven weight distribution. Halt crooked. Disturbance caused by rider moving seat.
Turn around the forehand.	Suppleness. Obedience to one-sided aids.	Straighten neck in front of shoulders. Keep moving fluently.	Stepping forward. Running. Hesitation. Inside hind leg moves alongside, instead of crossing in front of outside one.
Rein-back.	*Durchlaessigkeit.* Collection.	Think forward when starting movement.	Pulling. Running. Hesitation.
Half-volte returning to track. Turn around the quarters.	Collection.	Think forward. Correct lateral flexion in poll and lateral bend into direction of turn.	Wrong flexion. Quarters falling out. Inside hind leg escaping inwards. Horse stepping backwards.

Exercise	Purpose of Exercise	Tips for Execution of Exercise	Most Common Faults
Strike-off in named canter from walk.	Collection. Obedience.	Don't forget preparation with lateral flexion in poll. Important to align forehand with quarters.	Not forward enough. Quarters falling in.
Simple change of leg at canter.	*Durchlaessigkeit.* Obedience.	Only a few, but definite, walking steps.	Lacking preparation for downward transition, therefore on forehand or via trot. Too many steps. Blurred transition to canter because of poor preparation.
Transition working canter-medium canter-collected canter.	*Durchlaessigkeit.* Collection. 'Schwung'.	Definite straightening. Collected canter with slight inward flexion in the poll.	Not enough forward riding, especially in transition to collected pace. Therefore loss of rhythm.

Voltes in collected trot and collected canter.	Collection. Straightness.	Use weight, leg and rein aids. Do not turn too sharply into volte.	Turning off too suddenly. Volte not round. Too much inside rein. Too little easing of outside rein. Lacking support of outside leg.

3. Basic Training for Jumping and Cross-Country Riding

Every horse should be quiet and safe to ride in the country, in traffic, and in the company of other horses.

Only after basic training has been consolidated should a horse start to specialize in either one or several disciplines of equestrian sport.

Jump training and riding across country are an integral part of any basic training. In the first phase of training, when familiarizing the horse with his surroundings, the trainer should take him out of doors. Difficulties and tensions often experienced in the indoor school or enclosed manège, nearly always disappear in suitable outdoor surroundings.

Along with gymnastic dressage training should go the familiarizing of the horse with his surroundings, and with various jumps and cross-country hazards including water. Apart from the fact that a horse is a lot more useful when he is manageable in every situation, the cross-country work also firms up tendons, ligaments, and joints.

When there is little possibility of regularly working a horse out of doors, cavaletti and gymnastic jumping are the best substitutes.

3(1) Cavaletti Work

Young horses are worked over cavaletti to acquaint them with obstructions on the ground; to help them to be more surefooted; and to make them supple and relaxed. For this purpose, single poles and low cavaletti should be distributed throughout the arena.

Their next function is to improve the rhythm and

length of stride. To achieve this, a row of cavaletti is put up, starting with two and three, later on increasing to six. The distance depends on the horse's natural length of stride. In general, the distance for horses in walk would be 0.80 metres (2½ft), for trot 1.3m (4′3″) and for canter 3.50m (11½ft). It is practical to place the cavaletti where they can be approached from several angles. If they are put on a circle they have to be closer to each other towards the centre and wider apart towards the outside. This

Cavaletti work at walk

Cavaletti work at trot

arrangement on a circle arc provides the option of varying distances to ride over. If enough material is available, cavaletti can be arranged at various places throughout the school, each arrangement at a different distance, so that riders can work at a variety of paces without having to move the cavaletti.

When the young horse has learned to trot over single poles on a long rein with a long and low neck, he can then work over a row of cavaletti. Maintaining an even and light contact, the rider should allow the horse to lower his head forwards/downwards by moving hands and arms along the sides of the horse's neck towards his mouth. (The horse should wear a neck strap, which the rider can catch if the horse should throw a sudden jump over the poles.)

During the approach, the rider has to establish and maintain a rhythmic working trot, otherwise the horse cannot cope with the distances between the cavaletti. It may be that the tempo will have to be slowed down with the reins while approaching the cavaletti. But this may only be done up to 3 metres (10 feet) before the first pole, then the hands must maintain only a light contact. It is not correct to drop the contact completely, as the horse would lose his rhythm.

If an impetuous horse is allowed to approach fast, he will jump into the cavaletti, lose confidence, and also risk injuring itself. Such a horse has to be calmed down by other means, such as the voice, or approaching on a circle, away from the stable or away from the other horses.

For safety reasons the trainer must avoid making the distances between the cavaletti too long – for instance, with the intention of lengthening the stride, which could easily cause the horse to injure his fetlock joints or sesamoid bones.

When working a young horse over cavaletti it is essential for the rider to ease his weight on the horse's back. The stirrups must be shortened to guarantee a balanced light seat. Praising a young horse during and after crossing

Cavaletti work on the lunge

At walk   At trot

the cavaletti will help him to understand and enjoy his work.

Lungeing over cavaletti has to be done with care, as the lunge could get wrapped around a side-cross of the cavaletti. A pole can be placed on top of the inside row of crosses, and another one leading up to the first cross.

Work over cavaletti is most profitable if it is repeated several times during the normal daily work. However, practising continuously and using cavaletti excessively will not improve performance; it is very strenuous for the horse, who can easily become tired or bored, and risk injuring himself.

3(2) Loose Jumping

When the young horse is surefooted and performs willingly over the row of cavaletti, maintaining rhythm and balance throughout, the jump training under the rider can begin. But before this an additional preparation is loose jumping. This is also a good remedy when retraining older horses which have been spoiled by bad riders or badly-built fences. In loose jumping they can recover their confidence and learn to enjoy themselves.

Suitable facilities are an indoor school or a manège with a high fence or a *couloir* (an outside jumping lane), often with fixed fences. On the inside this barrier must be low enough for the trainer to be able to push the horse on with the lungeing whip. Doors must be closed, and mirrors should be covered.

First, the young horse has to learn to move around the arena calmly and fluently, without jumping any fences at all. Then he is started with one small, inviting fence about 20–30cm (8 to 12in.) high. A cross-pole is an inviting fence. It also teaches the horse to jump in the centre. Otherwise a low pole with a ground line can be used. As the horse becomes accustomed to going round, jumping the first fence calmly and correctly balanced, more fences can gradually be added, one at a time, of varied design with varying numbers of non-jumping strides between each. Every loose jumping session should start off with a basic single fence.

Jumps up to 70–80cm (27 to 31in.) high may be fixed; higher fences must not be fixed.

The type of fences and the distances used depend on the purpose of the exercise.

Longish distances and sloping spread fences teach the horse to open up and stretch forward. Shorter-than-normal distances and upright fences or square oxers cause the horse to shorten his stride and to exert himself. For fluent jumping, the distances used should suit the natural stride of the individual horse the average stride being 3.20m to 3.60m (10½ to 12ft) long.

During the first few loose jumping sessions the horse should be jumped without a saddle; boots or bandages, however, should always be used. The bridle reins must be well secured by twisting them five to six times under the horse's neck and catching one rein loop with the throat lash. Later on the horse should be fully tacked, to familiarize him with the sudden tight feeling of girth and saddle when jumping. The stirrups should be removed, and the saddle flaps kept down by a surcingle.

The trainer will need at least two assistants: one to lead the horse into the jumping lane and one to welcome him when his rounds are finished. With sensible use of the lunge whip the trainer must teach the horse to maintain the necessary tempo. The assistant leading the horse into the lane must not interfere but must let go in time. The second assistant should have rewards ready and should call the horse in when he has finished. Horses understand this very quickly and respond willingly.

If several horses have to be jumped it is practical to have them brought into the school one after another, in order of similarity of their length of stride. Each horse should be first allowed to have some free exercise in the centre of the ring. This will get his circulation in motion. It is not good to bring a horse out of the stable and to start jumping straight away, which would undermine confidence and increase the risk of set fast.

When loose jumping is performed correctly and regularly, horses improve quickly. They learn to enjoy it and to find out for themselves the correct take-off points for various types of fence.

When a horse is jumping loose it is very important for everything to be peaceful and quiet. Shouting, cracking the whip, or chasing the horse around the school shows that the person in charge lacks knowledge.

3(3) Gymnastic Jumping

Along with dressage, jumping should be the main gymnastic exercise in the horse's training.

In gymnastic jumping the horse is trained over small fences of various types placed at various distances to make up different rows of jump sequences. This is the most comprehensive way of training a horse for a jumping career, as he will learn:

□ To use his back which develops his back muscles.
□ To develop the propulsive force of his quarters.
□ To find the correct take-off point by himself.
□ To develop and perfect his jumping style.
□ To gain confidence.
□ To react quickly.

There are a great number of exercises to choose from, the choice depending on the horse's specific requirements.

The basic exercise would be the regular use of inviting, small fences placed at distances suitable for the individual horse's stride. It is the rider's responsibility to maintain an even pace between the jumps. The suitable tempo is based on the natural pace of the horse. Any influence by the rider should come mainly from forward driving aids, with regulating rein aids playing a very secondary and supportive role.

In developing a horse's style and confidence jumping *from trot* is most beneficial. After a few trotting poles (distance 1.20m–1.30m or 4ft–4ft 3in.) a jump should be placed at a distance of 5m (16ft) after the last trotting pole. The horse has to trot over the poles in a calm but supple and impulsive trot, keeping his neck low and his nose pointing forwards/downwards. He must trot like this not only over the poles but also approaching the fence.

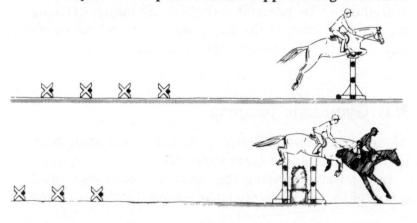

He should take off energetically, without rushing. Over the jump he should be confident and should round his back (*bascule*). He should maintain this approach even when the fence is adjusted into a spread, and widened.

Another even more intensive exercise along the same lines is work over a trotting pole, and 2.50m (8ft) behind it a small fence with the following fences at 3–3.50m or 10–11ft, their height increasing towards the end of the row. This work is extremely effective: it engages the horse's quarters, as he has to kick off again immediately after landing (in-and-out).

To teach the horse to look for and to find the correct take-off point, remove the second from last fence each time, thus increasing the number of non-jumping strides at the approach to the last fence.

To improve a horse's jumping technique the non-jumping strides can be shortened or lengthened between fences. Shorter distances teach the horse to gather himself before a fence and to lift his forehand. Longer distances teach the horse to energetically lengthen his stride and to kick off with determination at take-off.

To improve the horse's self confidence and to increase his ability to 'open up' over a fence, the trainer should progressively increase the width of a series of low spread fences.

Placing the row of fences on a large circle improves the horse's obedience and lateral flexion. It also improves the technique of his inside foreleg and hind leg.

The jumping conditions necessary for the success of gymnastic jumping are:
☐ It should be done regularly and progressively.
☐ The horse should concentrate and remain calm but forward-moving.
☐ The rider should have a balanced and supple seat and should ride with feel.

This jump training should be interspersed with further dressage training to prepare the horse for more advanced jumping. The jump training programme should be developed not by raising the heights of the fences but by frequently introducing small obstacles of novel design which are unfamiliar to the horse; and by varying the distances between them.

The trainer must constantly remember to plan the jump training carefully so as to avoid resistance, surprises, and allied problems. There should never be avoidable confrontations or battles of will between a horse and his trainer.

3(4) Course Jumping

When the horse is well trained in gymnastic jumping and can jump single, slightly larger, fences well and confidently, training can be extended to include jumping a course of fences. This will involve:

☐ Developing the horse's stamina.
☐ Jumping a course of fences at a set speed of 350 metres or 382 yards per minute.
☐ Jumping fences of different types and colours, fluently, economically and faultlessly.
☐ Riding changes of direction with the minimum of energy and with maximum effect.

Each course jumped should be used to assess the horse's obedience and its ability to canter and jump effectively.

To begin with, practice should be over only part of a course of small fences: the main objective being to maintain an even rhythm from start to finish. The rider must have sufficient feel and experience to establish the necessary basic speed for jumping each individual horse. Only later may the tempo be increased over short distances.

Going to horse shows and participating in carefully selected competitions gives the young horse a chance to get used to strange surroundings, music, crowds and other distractions. At the same time the trainer should assess the horse's nervous disposition and temperament, which may influence or possibly change his future training programme.

It is important to choose suitable competitions, especially on the first few outings. This will give the young horse a fair chance and enough time to become acquainted with his new circumstances.

Warming up has to be carried out calmly and thoroughly. To warm up and supple the horse's joints and muscles a lot of practise in working trot interspersed with short canter periods is necessary.

After the horse has settled and relaxed, a low practice fence should be jumped several times. Only towards the end of the warming up period should a few fences be jumped at competition height. The rider must remember that the warming up arena is not the place in which to train the horse. It merely gives him the opportunity of making a few well planned preparations for the competition.

While negotiating the course the rider *must concentrate*. His eyes should always be on the next fence. Even if the horse makes a mistake, the rider must never turn around and look at the fence to check if it has fallen down. This distraction might contribute towards a fault at the next fence.

Generally the rider should make a habit of entering and leaving the arena at a relaxed walk.

3(5) Cross-Country Training

Most of the instruction for the training of horse and rider across country has been given in Section 1 of this book.

When training a young horse, the best preparation for cross-country work is riding out often and calmly – where possible in the company of older, quiet horses. This way the horse learns to maintain his balance and confidence when going uphill, downhill, over uneven ground, and through dry ditches and shallow water. The young horse thus becomes relaxed and surefooted.

4. Training Horses with Bad Conformation and Difficult Temperament

Nowadays, because of selective breeding, it is rare to meet a horse with serious conformation faults or inborn bad temperament. When one does come across such a horse it is necessary to train him with extreme patience.

Complete relaxation and suppleness in a horse are the pre-requisites for any corrections. Since faulty conformation of limbs can hardly be influenced by riding, problems will mostly relate to the back or the set of head and neck.

Back too long
Too long a back – especially when it occurs in conjunction with weak loins – makes it difficult for the hind legs to come underneath the horse's body and closer to his centre of gravity. The hind legs seem to be dragged. Such a horse should only be worked in an outline, as for hacking.

Back too short
A back which is too short is difficult to make supple. The horse is hard to sit on, and there is a danger of putting stress on his legs. Short horses have to be ridden with a long, not too low, outline, trying to get the back to move elastically. In the long term cavaletti, gymnastic jumping and riding out of doors will improve the horse.

Over-built horses
An over-built horse is higher in the croup than in the withers. He is thus difficult to collect, and the ride feels

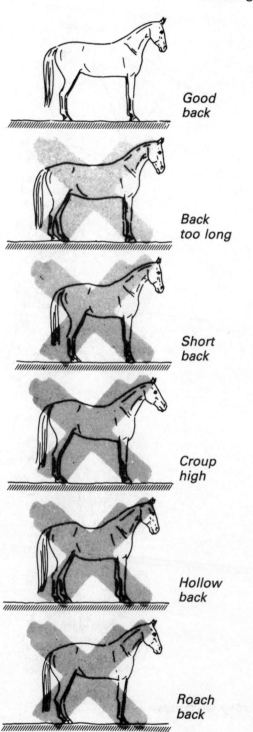

Good
back

Back
too long

Short
back

Croup
high

Hollow
back

Roach
back

Long
croup

Round
croup

Sloping
croup

Short
croup

Well-set head and neck

Swan neck

Low-set neck

Ewe neck

Short, thick neck with heavy jawbones

like riding 'downhill'. Patience and long term gymnastic exercising of the joints of the hind quarters must be employed. Over-built horses often have long, straight hind legs, which makes them difficult to bend.

Bad neck

An incorrectly muscled neck can be reshaped through long-term, specialized training. Sometimes the correct use of various auxiliary reins (side reins, running reins) can be helpful.

A badly set head will leave very little room between jaw bone and neck muscle. Under no circumstances must the rider try to put such a horse on the bit, but must first ride him in a long and low outline, until a better position of the lower neck muscle is achieved.

Faulty temperament

Faults in temperament are much more difficult to correct. They are often the result of incorrect training or handling in the preliminary stages, or from overfacing a horse at the beginning of his competitive career. Because the horse is afraid and feels insecure he seems to be excitable and erratic. The trainer must determine the underlying causes of such an unhappy situation. A reasoned approach is the best way of achieving a satisfactory remedy.

If a horse is born with a bad temperament he should only be ridden – if at all – by very experienced riders.

Index